C-4020   CAREER EXAMINATION SERIES

This is your
PASSBOOK for...

Court Revenue Assistant

Test Preparation Study Guide
Questions & Answers

COPYRIGHT NOTICE

This book is SOLELY intended for, is sold ONLY to, and its use is RESTRICTED to individual, bona fide applicants or candidates who qualify by virtue of having seriously filed applications for appropriate license, certificate, professional and/or promotional advancement, higher school matriculation, scholarship, or other legitimate requirements of education and/or governmental authorities.

This book is NOT intended for use, class instruction, tutoring, training, duplication, copying, reprinting, excerption, or adaptation, etc., by:

1) Other publishers
2) Proprietors and/or Instructors of "Coaching" and/or Preparatory Courses
3) Personnel and/or Training Divisions of commercial, industrial, and governmental organizations
4) Schools, colleges, or universities and/or their departments and staffs, including teachers and other personnel
5) Testing Agencies or Bureaus
6) Study groups which seek by the purchase of a single volume to copy and/or duplicate and/or adapt this material for use by the group as a whole without having purchased individual volumes for each of the members of the group
7) Et al.

Such persons would be in violation of appropriate Federal and State statutes.

PROVISION OF LICENSING AGREEMENTS – Recognized educational, commercial, industrial, and governmental institutions and organizations, and others legitimately engaged in educational pursuits, including training, testing, and measurement activities, may address request for a licensing agreement to the copyright owners, who will determine whether, and under what conditions, including fees and charges, the materials in this book may be used them. In other words, a licensing facility exists for the legitimate use of the material in this book on other than an individual basis. However, it is asseverated and affirmed here that the material in this book CANNOT be used without the receipt of the express permission of such a licensing agreement from the Publishers. Inquiries re licensing should be addressed to the company, attention rights and permissions department.

All rights reserved, including the right of reproduction in whole or in part, in any form or by any means, electronic or mechanical, including photocopying, recording, or by any information storage and retrieval system, without permission in writing from the Publisher.

Copyright © 2024 by
National Learning Corporation

212 Michael Drive, Syosset, NY 11791
(516) 921-8888 • www.passbooks.com
E-mail: info@passbooks.com

PUBLISHED IN THE UNITED STATES OF AMERICA

PASSBOOK® SERIES

THE *PASSBOOK® SERIES* has been created to prepare applicants and candidates for the ultimate academic battlefield – the examination room.

At some time in our lives, each and every one of us may be required to take an examination – for validation, matriculation, admission, qualification, registration, certification, or licensure.

Based on the assumption that every applicant or candidate has met the basic formal educational standards, has taken the required number of courses, and read the necessary texts, the *PASSBOOK® SERIES* furnishes the one special preparation which may assure passing with confidence, instead of failing with insecurity. Examination questions – together with answers – are furnished as the basic vehicle for study so that the mysteries of the examination and its compounding difficulties may be eliminated or diminished by a sure method.

This book is meant to help you pass your examination provided that you qualify and are serious in your objective.

The entire field is reviewed through the huge store of content information which is succinctly presented through a provocative and challenging approach – the question-and-answer method.

A climate of success is established by furnishing the correct answers at the end of each test.

You soon learn to recognize types of questions, forms of questions, and patterns of questioning. You may even begin to anticipate expected outcomes.

You perceive that many questions are repeated or adapted so that you can gain acute insights, which may enable you to score many sure points.

You learn how to confront new questions, or types of questions, and to attack them confidently and work out the correct answers.

You note objectives and emphases, and recognize pitfalls and dangers, so that you may make positive educational adjustments.

Moreover, you are kept fully informed in relation to new concepts, methods, practices, and directions in the field.

You discover that you are actually taking the examination all the time: you are preparing for the examination by "taking" an examination, not by reading extraneous and/or supererogatory textbooks.

In short, this PASSBOOK®, used directedly, should be an important factor in helping you to pass your test.

COURT REVENUE ASSISTANT

DUTIES

Under direct supervision of a Chief Clerk, Deputy Chief Clerk or other supervisory personnel, Court Revenue Assistants serve as cashiers performing fiscal tasks in which mathematical calculations are fundamental including accepting fees, fines, bail or other payments; disbursing funds including the refund of bail, and performing daily cash drawer and monthly bank statement reconciliations. Court Revenue Assistants may also perform a variety of office clerical and administrative support tasks, such as checking, filing, and sorting court papers, obtaining and copying information, retrieving material from files, providing information at public counters, and other related duties.

SCOPE OF THE EXAMINATION

The written examination will consist of multiple-choice questions designed to assess the following:

1. **Coding and Decoding Information** - These questions assess a candidate's ability to use written sets of directions to code and decode information for court record keeping. Candidates will be presented with tabular information including names and numbers, and asked to apply a set of coding rules to encode information accurately. Candidates may be required to combine and reorganize the information to answer questions.
2. **Applying Facts and Information to Given Situations** - These questions assess a candidate's ability to use the information provided and apply it to a specific situation defined by a given set of facts. Each question contains a brief paragraph which describes a regulation, policy or procedure similar to what a Court Revenue Assistant may encounter on the job. All of the information to answer the questions is contained in the paragraph and in the description of the situation.
3. **Number Facility** - These questions require candidates to perform basic calculations involving addition, subtraction, multiplication, division and percentages. Information is presented in numerical or tabular format using forms typically found in the court setting.
4. **Reconciling Cash Balances** - These questions require candidates to work with various types of cash register summary reports. The candidates will be asked questions based solely on the information contained in these reports.
5. **Basic Legal and Revenue Collection Terminology** - These questions assess a candidate's knowledge of legal and revenue collection terminology and general court procedures that Court Revenue Assistants encounter in their daily work.
6. **Quality Service Orientation** - These questions assess a candidate's ability to respond to situations that Court Revenue Assistants encounter when interacting with the public and other court users.

HOW TO TAKE A TEST

I. YOU MUST PASS AN EXAMINATION

A. *WHAT EVERY CANDIDATE SHOULD KNOW*

Examination applicants often ask us for help in preparing for the written test. What can I study in advance? What kinds of questions will be asked? How will the test be given? How will the papers be graded?

As an applicant for a civil service examination, you may be wondering about some of these things. Our purpose here is to suggest effective methods of advance study and to describe civil service examinations.

Your chances for success on this examination can be increased if you know how to prepare. Those "pre-examination jitters" can be reduced if you know what to expect. You can even experience an adventure in good citizenship if you know why civil service exams are given.

B. *WHY ARE CIVIL SERVICE EXAMINATIONS GIVEN?*

Civil service examinations are important to you in two ways. As a citizen, you want public jobs filled by employees who know how to do their work. As a job seeker, you want a fair chance to compete for that job on an equal footing with other candidates. The best-known means of accomplishing this two-fold goal is the competitive examination.

Exams are widely publicized throughout the nation. They may be administered for jobs in federal, state, city, municipal, town or village governments or agencies.

Any citizen may apply, with some limitations, such as the age or residence of applicants. Your experience and education may be reviewed to see whether you meet the requirements for the particular examination. When these requirements exist, they are reasonable and applied consistently to all applicants. Thus, a competitive examination may cause you some uneasiness now, but it is your privilege and safeguard.

C. *HOW ARE CIVIL SERVICE EXAMS DEVELOPED?*

Examinations are carefully written by trained technicians who are specialists in the field known as "psychological measurement," in consultation with recognized authorities in the field of work that the test will cover. These experts recommend the subject matter areas or skills to be tested; only those knowledges or skills important to your success on the job are included. The most reliable books and source materials available are used as references. Together, the experts and technicians judge the difficulty level of the questions.

Test technicians know how to phrase questions so that the problem is clearly stated. Their ethics do not permit "trick" or "catch" questions. Questions may have been tried out on sample groups, or subjected to statistical analysis, to determine their usefulness.

Written tests are often used in combination with performance tests, ratings of training and experience, and oral interviews. All of these measures combine to form the best-known means of finding the right person for the right job.

II. HOW TO PASS THE WRITTEN TEST

A. NATURE OF THE EXAMINATION

To prepare intelligently for civil service examinations, you should know how they differ from school examinations you have taken. In school you were assigned certain definite pages to read or subjects to cover. The examination questions were quite detailed and usually emphasized memory. Civil service exams, on the other hand, try to discover your present ability to perform the duties of a position, plus your potentiality to learn these duties. In other words, a civil service exam attempts to predict how successful you will be. Questions cover such a broad area that they cannot be as minute and detailed as school exam questions.

In the public service similar kinds of work, or positions, are grouped together in one "class." This process is known as *position-classification*. All the positions in a class are paid according to the salary range for that class. One class title covers all of these positions, and they are all tested by the same examination.

B. FOUR BASIC STEPS

1) Study the announcement

How, then, can you know what subjects to study? Our best answer is: "Learn as much as possible about the class of positions for which you've applied." The exam will test the knowledge, skills and abilities needed to do the work.

Your most valuable source of information about the position you want is the official exam announcement. This announcement lists the training and experience qualifications. Check these standards and apply only if you come reasonably close to meeting them.

The brief description of the position in the examination announcement offers some clues to the subjects which will be tested. Think about the job itself. Review the duties in your mind. Can you perform them, or are there some in which you are rusty? Fill in the blank spots in your preparation.

Many jurisdictions preview the written test in the exam announcement by including a section called "Knowledge and Abilities Required," "Scope of the Examination," or some similar heading. Here you will find out specifically what fields will be tested.

2) Review your own background

Once you learn in general what the position is all about, and what you need to know to do the work, ask yourself which subjects you already know fairly well and which need improvement. You may wonder whether to concentrate on improving your strong areas or on building some background in your fields of weakness. When the announcement has specified "some knowledge" or "considerable knowledge," or has used adjectives like "beginning principles of…" or "advanced … methods," you can get a clue as to the number and difficulty of questions to be asked in any given field. More questions, and hence broader coverage, would be included for those subjects which are more important in the work. Now weigh your strengths and weaknesses against the job requirements and prepare accordingly.

3) Determine the level of the position

Another way to tell how intensively you should prepare is to understand the level of the job for which you are applying. Is it the entering level? In other words, is this the position in which beginners in a field of work are hired? Or is it an intermediate or advanced level? Sometimes this is indicated by such words as "Junior" or "Senior" in the class title. Other jurisdictions use Roman numerals to designate the level – Clerk I, Clerk II, for example. The word "Supervisor" sometimes appears in the title. If the level is not indicated by the title, check the description of duties. Will you be working under very close supervision, or will you have responsibility for independent decisions in this work?

4) Choose appropriate study materials

Now that you know the subjects to be examined and the relative amount of each subject to be covered, you can choose suitable study materials. For beginning level jobs, or even advanced ones, if you have a pronounced weakness in some aspect of your training, read a modern, standard textbook in that field. Be sure it is up to date and has general coverage. Such books are normally available at your library, and the librarian will be glad to help you locate one. For entry-level positions, questions of appropriate difficulty are chosen – neither highly advanced questions, nor those too simple. Such questions require careful thought but not advanced training.

If the position for which you are applying is technical or advanced, you will read more advanced, specialized material. If you are already familiar with the basic principles of your field, elementary textbooks would waste your time. Concentrate on advanced textbooks and technical periodicals. Think through the concepts and review difficult problems in your field.

These are all general sources. You can get more ideas on your own initiative, following these leads. For example, training manuals and publications of the government agency which employs workers in your field can be useful, particularly for technical and professional positions. A letter or visit to the government department involved may result in more specific study suggestions, and certainly will provide you with a more definite idea of the exact nature of the position you are seeking.

III. KINDS OF TESTS

Tests are used for purposes other than measuring knowledge and ability to perform specified duties. For some positions, it is equally important to test ability to make adjustments to new situations or to profit from training. In others, basic mental abilities not dependent on information are essential. Questions which test these things may not appear as pertinent to the duties of the position as those which test for knowledge and information. Yet they are often highly important parts of a fair examination. For very general questions, it is almost impossible to help you direct your study efforts. What we can do is to point out some of the more common of these general abilities needed in public service positions and describe some typical questions.

1) General information

Broad, general information has been found useful for predicting job success in some kinds of work. This is tested in a variety of ways, from vocabulary lists to questions about current events. Basic background in some field of work, such as sociology or economics, may be sampled in a group of questions. Often these are principles which have become familiar to most persons through exposure rather than through formal training. It is difficult to advise you how to study for these questions; being alert to the world around you is our best suggestion.

2) Verbal ability

An example of an ability needed in many positions is verbal or language ability. Verbal ability is, in brief, the ability to use and understand words. Vocabulary and grammar tests are typical measures of this ability. Reading comprehension or paragraph interpretation questions are common in many kinds of civil service tests. You are given a paragraph of written material and asked to find its central meaning.

3) Numerical ability

Number skills can be tested by the familiar arithmetic problem, by checking paired lists of numbers to see which are alike and which are different, or by interpreting charts and graphs. In the latter test, a graph may be printed in the test booklet which you are asked to use as the basis for answering questions.

4) Observation

A popular test for law-enforcement positions is the observation test. A picture is shown to you for several minutes, then taken away. Questions about the picture test your ability to observe both details and larger elements.

5) Following directions

In many positions in the public service, the employee must be able to carry out written instructions dependably and accurately. You may be given a chart with several columns, each column listing a variety of information. The questions require you to carry out directions involving the information given in the chart.

6) Skills and aptitudes

Performance tests effectively measure some manual skills and aptitudes. When the skill is one in which you are trained, such as typing or shorthand, you can practice. These tests are often very much like those given in business school or high school courses. For many of the other skills and aptitudes, however, no short-time preparation can be made. Skills and abilities natural to you or that you have developed throughout your lifetime are being tested.

Many of the general questions just described provide all the data needed to answer the questions and ask you to use your reasoning ability to find the answers. Your best preparation for these tests, as well as for tests of facts and ideas, is to be at your physical and mental best. You, no doubt, have your own methods of getting into an exam-taking mood and keeping "in shape." The next section lists some ideas on this subject.

IV. KINDS OF QUESTIONS

Only rarely is the "essay" question, which you answer in narrative form, used in civil service tests. Civil service tests are usually of the short-answer type. Full instructions for answering these questions will be given to you at the examination. But in case this is your first experience with short-answer questions and separate answer sheets, here is what you need to know:

1) Multiple-choice Questions

Most popular of the short-answer questions is the "multiple choice" or "best answer" question. It can be used, for example, to test for factual knowledge, ability to solve problems or judgment in meeting situations found at work.

A multiple-choice question is normally one of three types—
- It can begin with an incomplete statement followed by several possible endings. You are to find the one ending which *best* completes the statement, although some of the others may not be entirely wrong.
- It can also be a complete statement in the form of a question which is answered by choosing one of the statements listed.

- It can be in the form of a problem – again you select the best answer.

Here is an example of a multiple-choice question with a discussion which should give you some clues as to the method for choosing the right answer:

When an employee has a complaint about his assignment, the action which will *best* help him overcome his difficulty is to
- A. discuss his difficulty with his coworkers
- B. take the problem to the head of the organization
- C. take the problem to the person who gave him the assignment
- D. say nothing to anyone about his complaint

In answering this question, you should study each of the choices to find which is best. Consider choice "A" – Certainly an employee may discuss his complaint with fellow employees, but no change or improvement can result, and the complaint remains unresolved. Choice "B" is a poor choice since the head of the organization probably does not know what assignment you have been given, and taking your problem to him is known as "going over the head" of the supervisor. The supervisor, or person who made the assignment, is the person who can clarify it or correct any injustice. Choice "C" is, therefore, correct. To say nothing, as in choice "D," is unwise. Supervisors have and interest in knowing the problems employees are facing, and the employee is seeking a solution to his problem.

2) True/False Questions

The "true/false" or "right/wrong" form of question is sometimes used. Here a complete statement is given. Your job is to decide whether the statement is right or wrong.

SAMPLE: A roaming cell-phone call to a nearby city costs less than a non-roaming call to a distant city.

This statement is wrong, or false, since roaming calls are more expensive.

This is not a complete list of all possible question forms, although most of the others are variations of these common types. You will always get complete directions for answering questions. Be sure you understand *how* to mark your answers – ask questions until you do.

V. RECORDING YOUR ANSWERS

Computer terminals are used more and more today for many different kinds of exams.

For an examination with very few applicants, you may be told to record your answers in the test booklet itself. Separate answer sheets are much more common. If this separate answer sheet is to be scored by machine – and this is often the case – it is highly important that you mark your answers correctly in order to get credit.

An electronic scoring machine is often used in civil service offices because of the speed with which papers can be scored. Machine-scored answer sheets must be marked with a pencil, which will be given to you. This pencil has a high graphite content which responds to the electronic scoring machine. As a matter of fact, stray dots may register as answers, so do not let your pencil rest on the answer sheet while you are pondering the correct answer. Also, if your pencil lead breaks or is otherwise defective, ask for another.

Since the answer sheet will be dropped in a slot in the scoring machine, be careful not to bend the corners or get the paper crumpled.

The answer sheet normally has five vertical columns of numbers, with 30 numbers to a column. These numbers correspond to the question numbers in your test booklet. After each number, going across the page are four or five pairs of dotted lines. These short dotted lines have small letters or numbers above them. The first two pairs may also have a "T" or "F" above the letters. This indicates that the first two pairs only are to be used if the questions are of the true-false type. If the questions are multiple choice, disregard the "T" and "F" and pay attention only to the small letters or numbers.

Answer your questions in the manner of the sample that follows:

32. The largest city in the United States is
    A. Washington, D.C.
    B. New York City
    C. Chicago
    D. Detroit
    E. San Francisco

1) Choose the answer you think is best. (New York City is the largest, so "B" is correct.)
2) Find the row of dotted lines numbered the same as the question you are answering. (Find row number 32)
3) Find the pair of dotted lines corresponding to the answer. (Find the pair of lines under the mark "B.")
4) Make a solid black mark between the dotted lines.

VI. BEFORE THE TEST

Common sense will help you find procedures to follow to get ready for an examination. Too many of us, however, overlook these sensible measures. Indeed, nervousness and fatigue have been found to be the most serious reasons why applicants fail to do their best on civil service tests. Here is a list of reminders:

- Begin your preparation early – Don't wait until the last minute to go scurrying around for books and materials or to find out what the position is all about.
- Prepare continuously – An hour a night for a week is better than an all-night cram session. This has been definitely established. What is more, a night a week for a month will return better dividends than crowding your study into a shorter period of time.
- Locate the place of the exam – You have been sent a notice telling you when and where to report for the examination. If the location is in a different town or otherwise unfamiliar to you, it would be well to inquire the best route and learn something about the building.
- Relax the night before the test – Allow your mind to rest. Do not study at all that night. Plan some mild recreation or diversion; then go to bed early and get a good night's sleep.
- Get up early enough to make a leisurely trip to the place for the test – This way unforeseen events, traffic snarls, unfamiliar buildings, etc. will not upset you.
- Dress comfortably – A written test is not a fashion show. You will be known by number and not by name, so wear something comfortable.

- Leave excess paraphernalia at home – Shopping bags and odd bundles will get in your way. You need bring only the items mentioned in the official notice you received; usually everything you need is provided. Do not bring reference books to the exam. They will only confuse those last minutes and be taken away from you when in the test room.
- Arrive somewhat ahead of time – If because of transportation schedules you must get there very early, bring a newspaper or magazine to take your mind off yourself while waiting.
- Locate the examination room – When you have found the proper room, you will be directed to the seat or part of the room where you will sit. Sometimes you are given a sheet of instructions to read while you are waiting. Do not fill out any forms until you are told to do so; just read them and be prepared.
- Relax and prepare to listen to the instructions
- If you have any physical problem that may keep you from doing your best, be sure to tell the test administrator. If you are sick or in poor health, you really cannot do your best on the exam. You can come back and take the test some other time.

VII. AT THE TEST

The day of the test is here and you have the test booklet in your hand. The temptation to get going is very strong. Caution! There is more to success than knowing the right answers. You must know how to identify your papers and understand variations in the type of short-answer question used in this particular examination. Follow these suggestions for maximum results from your efforts:

1) Cooperate with the monitor

The test administrator has a duty to create a situation in which you can be as much at ease as possible. He will give instructions, tell you when to begin, check to see that you are marking your answer sheet correctly, and so on. He is not there to guard you, although he will see that your competitors do not take unfair advantage. He wants to help you do your best.

2) Listen to all instructions

Don't jump the gun! Wait until you understand all directions. In most civil service tests you get more time than you need to answer the questions. So don't be in a hurry. Read each word of instructions until you clearly understand the meaning. Study the examples, listen to all announcements and follow directions. Ask questions if you do not understand what to do.

3) Identify your papers

Civil service exams are usually identified by number only. You will be assigned a number; you must not put your name on your test papers. Be sure to copy your number correctly. Since more than one exam may be given, copy your exact examination title.

4) Plan your time

Unless you are told that a test is a "speed" or "rate of work" test, speed itself is usually not important. Time enough to answer all the questions will be provided, but this does not mean that you have all day. An overall time limit has been set. Divide the total time (in minutes) by the number of questions to determine the approximate time you have for each question.

5) Do not linger over difficult questions

If you come across a difficult question, mark it with a paper clip (useful to have along) and come back to it when you have been through the booklet. One caution if you do this – be sure to skip a number on your answer sheet as well. Check often to be sure that you have not lost your place and that you are marking in the row numbered the same as the question you are answering.

6) Read the questions

Be sure you know what the question asks! Many capable people are unsuccessful because they failed to *read* the questions correctly.

7) Answer all questions

Unless you have been instructed that a penalty will be deducted for incorrect answers, it is better to guess than to omit a question.

8) Speed tests

It is often better NOT to guess on speed tests. It has been found that on timed tests people are tempted to spend the last few seconds before time is called in marking answers at random – without even reading them – in the hope of picking up a few extra points. To discourage this practice, the instructions may warn you that your score will be "corrected" for guessing. That is, a penalty will be applied. The incorrect answers will be deducted from the correct ones, or some other penalty formula will be used.

9) Review your answers

If you finish before time is called, go back to the questions you guessed or omitted to give them further thought. Review other answers if you have time.

10) Return your test materials

If you are ready to leave before others have finished or time is called, take ALL your materials to the monitor and leave quietly. Never take any test material with you. The monitor can discover whose papers are not complete, and taking a test booklet may be grounds for disqualification.

VIII. EXAMINATION TECHNIQUES

1) Read the general instructions carefully. These are usually printed on the first page of the exam booklet. As a rule, these instructions refer to the timing of the examination; the fact that you should not start work until the signal and must stop work at a signal, etc. If there are any *special* instructions, such as a choice of questions to be answered, make sure that you note this instruction carefully.

2) When you are ready to start work on the examination, that is as soon as the signal has been given, read the instructions to each question booklet, underline any key words or phrases, such as *least, best, outline, describe* and the like. In this way you will tend to answer as requested rather than discover on reviewing your paper that you *listed without describing*, that you selected the *worst* choice rather than the *best* choice, etc.

3) If the examination is of the objective or multiple-choice type – that is, each question will also give a series of possible answers: A, B, C or D, and you are called upon to select the best answer and write the letter next to that answer on your answer paper – it is advisable to start answering each question in turn. There may be anywhere from 50 to 100 such questions in the three or four hours allotted and you can see how much time would be taken if you read through all the questions before beginning to answer any. Furthermore, if you come across a question or group of questions which you know would be difficult to answer, it would undoubtedly affect your handling of all the other questions.

4) If the examination is of the essay type and contains but a few questions, it is a moot point as to whether you should read all the questions before starting to answer any one. Of course, if you are given a choice – say five out of seven and the like – then it is essential to read all the questions so you can eliminate the two that are most difficult. If, however, you are asked to answer all the questions, there may be danger in trying to answer the easiest one first because you may find that you will spend too much time on it. The best technique is to answer the first question, then proceed to the second, etc.

5) Time your answers. Before the exam begins, write down the time it started, then add the time allowed for the examination and write down the time it must be completed, then divide the time available somewhat as follows:
   - If 3-1/2 hours are allowed, that would be 210 minutes. If you have 80 objective-type questions, that would be an average of 2-1/2 minutes per question. Allow yourself no more than 2 minutes per question, or a total of 160 minutes, which will permit about 50 minutes to review.
   - If for the time allotment of 210 minutes there are 7 essay questions to answer, that would average about 30 minutes a question. Give yourself only 25 minutes per question so that you have about 35 minutes to review.

6) The most important instruction is to *read each question* and make sure you know what is wanted. The second most important instruction is to *time yourself properly* so that you answer every question. The third most important instruction is to *answer every question*. Guess if you have to but include something for each question. Remember that you will receive no credit for a blank and will probably receive some credit if you write something in answer to an essay question. If you guess a letter – say "B" for a multiple-choice question – you may have guessed right. If you leave a blank as an answer to a multiple-choice question, the examiners may respect your feelings but it will not add a point to your score. Some exams may penalize you for wrong answers, so in such cases *only*, you may not want to guess unless you have some basis for your answer.

7) Suggestions
   a. Objective-type questions
      1. Examine the question booklet for proper sequence of pages and questions
      2. Read all instructions carefully
      3. Skip any question which seems too difficult; return to it after all other questions have been answered
      4. Apportion your time properly; do not spend too much time on any single question or group of questions

5. Note and underline key words – *all, most, fewest, least, best, worst, same, opposite,* etc.
6. Pay particular attention to negatives
7. Note unusual option, e.g., unduly long, short, complex, different or similar in content to the body of the question
8. Observe the use of "hedging" words – *probably, may, most likely,* etc.
9. Make sure that your answer is put next to the same number as the question
10. Do not second-guess unless you have good reason to believe the second answer is definitely more correct
11. Cross out original answer if you decide another answer is more accurate; do not erase until you are ready to hand your paper in
12. Answer all questions; guess unless instructed otherwise
13. Leave time for review

  b. Essay questions
    1. Read each question carefully
    2. Determine exactly what is wanted. Underline key words or phrases.
    3. Decide on outline or paragraph answer
    4. Include many different points and elements unless asked to develop any one or two points or elements
    5. Show impartiality by giving pros and cons unless directed to select one side only
    6. Make and write down any assumptions you find necessary to answer the questions
    7. Watch your English, grammar, punctuation and choice of words
    8. Time your answers; don't crowd material

8) Answering the essay question

Most essay questions can be answered by framing the specific response around several key words or ideas. Here are a few such key words or ideas:

M's: manpower, materials, methods, money, management
P's: purpose, program, policy, plan, procedure, practice, problems, pitfalls, personnel, public relations

  a. Six basic steps in handling problems:
    1. Preliminary plan and background development
    2. Collect information, data and facts
    3. Analyze and interpret information, data and facts
    4. Analyze and develop solutions as well as make recommendations
    5. Prepare report and sell recommendations
    6. Install recommendations and follow up effectiveness

  b. Pitfalls to avoid
    1. *Taking things for granted* – A statement of the situation does not necessarily imply that each of the elements is necessarily true; for example, a complaint may be invalid and biased so that all that can be taken for granted is that a complaint has been registered

2. *Considering only one side of a situation* – Wherever possible, indicate several alternatives and then point out the reasons you selected the best one
3. *Failing to indicate follow up* – Whenever your answer indicates action on your part, make certain that you will take proper follow-up action to see how successful your recommendations, procedures or actions turn out to be
4. *Taking too long in answering any single question* – Remember to time your answers properly

IX. AFTER THE TEST

Scoring procedures differ in detail among civil service jurisdictions although the general principles are the same. Whether the papers are hand-scored or graded by machine we have described, they are nearly always graded by number. That is, the person who marks the paper knows only the number – never the name – of the applicant. Not until all the papers have been graded will they be matched with names. If other tests, such as training and experience or oral interview ratings have been given, scores will be combined. Different parts of the examination usually have different weights. For example, the written test might count 60 percent of the final grade, and a rating of training and experience 40 percent. In many jurisdictions, veterans will have a certain number of points added to their grades.

After the final grade has been determined, the names are placed in grade order and an eligible list is established. There are various methods for resolving ties between those who get the same final grade – probably the most common is to place first the name of the person whose application was received first. Job offers are made from the eligible list in the order the names appear on it. You will be notified of your grade and your rank as soon as all these computations have been made. This will be done as rapidly as possible.

People who are found to meet the requirements in the announcement are called "eligibles." Their names are put on a list of eligible candidates. An eligible's chances of getting a job depend on how high he stands on this list and how fast agencies are filling jobs from the list.

When a job is to be filled from a list of eligibles, the agency asks for the names of people on the list of eligibles for that job. When the civil service commission receives this request, it sends to the agency the names of the three people highest on this list. Or, if the job to be filled has specialized requirements, the office sends the agency the names of the top three persons who meet these requirements from the general list.

The appointing officer makes a choice from among the three people whose names were sent to him. If the selected person accepts the appointment, the names of the others are put back on the list to be considered for future openings.

That is the rule in hiring from all kinds of eligible lists, whether they are for typist, carpenter, chemist, or something else. For every vacancy, the appointing officer has his choice of any one of the top three eligibles on the list. This explains why the person whose name is on top of the list sometimes does not get an appointment when some of the persons lower on the list do. If the appointing officer chooses the second or third eligible, the No. 1 eligible does not get a job at once, but stays on the list until he is appointed or the list is terminated.

X. HOW TO PASS THE INTERVIEW TEST

The examination for which you applied requires an oral interview test. You have already taken the written test and you are now being called for the interview test – the final part of the formal examination.

You may think that it is not possible to prepare for an interview test and that there are no procedures to follow during an interview. Our purpose is to point out some things you can do in advance that will help you and some good rules to follow and pitfalls to avoid while you are being interviewed.

What is an interview supposed to test?

The written examination is designed to test the technical knowledge and competence of the candidate; the oral is designed to evaluate intangible qualities, not readily measured otherwise, and to establish a list showing the relative fitness of each candidate – as measured against his competitors – for the position sought. Scoring is not on the basis of "right" and "wrong," but on a sliding scale of values ranging from "not passable" to "outstanding." As a matter of fact, it is possible to achieve a relatively low score without a single "incorrect" answer because of evident weakness in the qualities being measured.

Occasionally, an examination may consist entirely of an oral test – either an individual or a group oral. In such cases, information is sought concerning the technical knowledges and abilities of the candidate, since there has been no written examination for this purpose. More commonly, however, an oral test is used to supplement a written examination.

Who conducts interviews?

The composition of oral boards varies among different jurisdictions. In nearly all, a representative of the personnel department serves as chairman. One of the members of the board may be a representative of the department in which the candidate would work. In some cases, "outside experts" are used, and, frequently, a businessman or some other representative of the general public is asked to serve. Labor and management or other special groups may be represented. The aim is to secure the services of experts in the appropriate field.

However the board is composed, it is a good idea (and not at all improper or unethical) to ascertain in advance of the interview who the members are and what groups they represent. When you are introduced to them, you will have some idea of their backgrounds and interests, and at least you will not stutter and stammer over their names.

What should be done before the interview?

While knowledge about the board members is useful and takes some of the surprise element out of the interview, there is other preparation which is more substantive. It *is* possible to prepare for an oral interview – in several ways:

1) Keep a copy of your application and review it carefully before the interview

This may be the only document before the oral board, and the starting point of the interview. Know what education and experience you have listed there, and the sequence and dates of all of it. Sometimes the board will ask you to review the highlights of your experience for them; you should not have to hem and haw doing it.

2) Study the class specification and the examination announcement

Usually, the oral board has one or both of these to guide them. The qualities, characteristics or knowledges required by the position sought are stated in these documents. They offer valuable clues as to the nature of the oral interview. For example, if the job involves supervisory responsibilities, the announcement will usually indicate that knowledge of modern supervisory methods and the qualifications of the candidate as a supervisor will be tested. If so, you can expect such questions, frequently in the form of a hypothetical situation which you are expected to solve. NEVER go into an oral without knowledge of the duties and responsibilities of the job you seek.

3) Think through each qualification required

Try to visualize the kind of questions you would ask if you were a board member. How well could you answer them? Try especially to appraise your own knowledge and background in each area, *measured against the job sought*, and identify any areas in which you are weak. Be critical and realistic – do not flatter yourself.

4) Do some general reading in areas in which you feel you may be weak

For example, if the job involves supervision and your past experience has NOT, some general reading in supervisory methods and practices, particularly in the field of human relations, might be useful. Do NOT study agency procedures or detailed manuals. The oral board will be testing your understanding and capacity, not your memory.

5) Get a good night's sleep and watch your general health and mental attitude

You will want a clear head at the interview. Take care of a cold or any other minor ailment, and of course, no hangovers.

What should be done on the day of the interview?

Now comes the day of the interview itself. Give yourself plenty of time to get there. Plan to arrive somewhat ahead of the scheduled time, particularly if your appointment is in the fore part of the day. If a previous candidate fails to appear, the board might be ready for you a bit early. By early afternoon an oral board is almost invariably behind schedule if there are many candidates, and you may have to wait. Take along a book or magazine to read, or your application to review, but leave any extraneous material in the waiting room when you go in for your interview. In any event, relax and compose yourself.

The matter of dress is important. The board is forming impressions about you – from your experience, your manners, your attitude, and your appearance. Give your personal appearance careful attention. Dress your best, but not your flashiest. Choose conservative, appropriate clothing, and be sure it is immaculate. This is a business interview, and your appearance should indicate that you regard it as such. Besides, being well groomed and properly dressed will help boost your confidence.

Sooner or later, someone will call your name and escort you into the interview room. *This is it.* From here on you are on your own. It is too late for any more preparation. But remember, you asked for this opportunity to prove your fitness, and you are here because your request was granted.

What happens when you go in?

The usual sequence of events will be as follows: The clerk (who is often the board stenographer) will introduce you to the chairman of the oral board, who will introduce you to the other members of the board. Acknowledge the introductions before you sit down. Do not be surprised if you find a microphone facing you or a stenotypist sitting by. Oral interviews are usually recorded in the event of an appeal or other review.

Usually the chairman of the board will open the interview by reviewing the highlights of your education and work experience from your application – primarily for the benefit of the other members of the board, as well as to get the material into the record. Do not interrupt or comment unless there is an error or significant misinterpretation; if that is the case, do not hesitate. But do not quibble about insignificant matters. Also, he will usually ask you some question about your education, experience or your present job – partly to get you to start talking and to establish the interviewing "rapport." He may start the actual questioning, or turn it over to one of the other members. Frequently, each member undertakes the questioning on a particular area, one in which he is perhaps most competent, so you can expect each member to participate in the examination. Because time is limited, you may also expect some rather abrupt switches in the direction the questioning takes, so do not be upset by it. Normally, a board member will not pursue a single line of questioning unless he discovers a particular strength or weakness.

After each member has participated, the chairman will usually ask whether any member has any further questions, then will ask you if you have anything you wish to add. Unless you are expecting this question, it may floor you. Worse, it may start you off on an extended, extemporaneous speech. The board is not usually seeking more information. The question is principally to offer you a last opportunity to present further qualifications or to indicate that you have nothing to add. So, if you feel that a significant qualification or characteristic has been overlooked, it is proper to point it out in a sentence or so. Do not compliment the board on the thoroughness of their examination – they have been sketchy, and you know it. If you wish, merely say, "No thank you, I have nothing further to add." This is a point where you can "talk yourself out" of a good impression or fail to present an important bit of information. Remember, *you close the interview yourself.*

The chairman will then say, "That is all, Mr. _____, thank you." Do not be startled; the interview is over, and quicker than you think. Thank him, gather your belongings and take your leave. Save your sigh of relief for the other side of the door.

How to put your best foot forward

Throughout this entire process, you may feel that the board individually and collectively is trying to pierce your defenses, seek out your hidden weaknesses and embarrass and confuse you. Actually, this is not true. They are obliged to make an appraisal of your qualifications for the job you are seeking, and they want to see you in your best light. Remember, they must interview all candidates and a non-cooperative candidate may become a failure in spite of their best efforts to bring out his qualifications. Here are 15 suggestions that will help you:

1) Be natural – Keep your attitude confident, not cocky

If you are not confident that you can do the job, do not expect the board to be. Do not apologize for your weaknesses, try to bring out your strong points. The board is interested in a positive, not negative, presentation. Cockiness will antagonize any board member and make him wonder if you are covering up a weakness by a false show of strength.

2) Get comfortable, but don't lounge or sprawl

Sit erectly but not stiffly. A careless posture may lead the board to conclude that you are careless in other things, or at least that you are not impressed by the importance of the occasion. Either conclusion is natural, even if incorrect. Do not fuss with your clothing, a pencil or an ashtray. Your hands may occasionally be useful to emphasize a point; do not let them become a point of distraction.

3) Do not wisecrack or make small talk

This is a serious situation, and your attitude should show that you consider it as such. Further, the time of the board is limited – they do not want to waste it, and neither should you.

4) Do not exaggerate your experience or abilities

In the first place, from information in the application or other interviews and sources, the board may know more about you than you think. Secondly, you probably will not get away with it. An experienced board is rather adept at spotting such a situation, so do not take the chance.

5) If you know a board member, do not make a point of it, yet do not hide it

Certainly you are not fooling him, and probably not the other members of the board. Do not try to take advantage of your acquaintanceship – it will probably do you little good.

6) Do not dominate the interview

Let the board do that. They will give you the clues – do not assume that you have to do all the talking. Realize that the board has a number of questions to ask you, and do not try to take up all the interview time by showing off your extensive knowledge of the answer to the first one.

7) Be attentive

You only have 20 minutes or so, and you should keep your attention at its sharpest throughout. When a member is addressing a problem or question to you, give him your undivided attention. Address your reply principally to him, but do not exclude the other board members.

8) Do not interrupt

A board member may be stating a problem for you to analyze. He will ask you a question when the time comes. Let him state the problem, and wait for the question.

9) Make sure you understand the question

Do not try to answer until you are sure what the question is. If it is not clear, restate it in your own words or ask the board member to clarify it for you. However, do not haggle about minor elements.

10) Reply promptly but not hastily

A common entry on oral board rating sheets is "candidate responded readily," or "candidate hesitated in replies." Respond as promptly and quickly as you can, but do not jump to a hasty, ill-considered answer.

11) Do not be peremptory in your answers

A brief answer is proper – but do not fire your answer back. That is a losing game from your point of view. The board member can probably ask questions much faster than you can answer them.

12) Do not try to create the answer you think the board member wants

He is interested in what kind of mind you have and how it works – not in playing games. Furthermore, he can usually spot this practice and will actually grade you down on it.

13) Do not switch sides in your reply merely to agree with a board member

Frequently, a member will take a contrary position merely to draw you out and to see if you are willing and able to defend your point of view. Do not start a debate, yet do not surrender a good position. If a position is worth taking, it is worth defending.

14) Do not be afraid to admit an error in judgment if you are shown to be wrong

The board knows that you are forced to reply without any opportunity for careful consideration. Your answer may be demonstrably wrong. If so, admit it and get on with the interview.

15) Do not dwell at length on your present job

The opening question may relate to your present assignment. Answer the question but do not go into an extended discussion. You are being examined for a *new* job, not your present one. As a matter of fact, try to phrase ALL your answers in terms of the job for which you are being examined.

Basis of Rating

Probably you will forget most of these "do's" and "don'ts" when you walk into the oral interview room. Even remembering them all will not ensure you a passing grade. Perhaps you did not have the qualifications in the first place. But remembering them will help you to put your best foot forward, without treading on the toes of the board members.

Rumor and popular opinion to the contrary notwithstanding, an oral board wants you to make the best appearance possible. They know you are under pressure – but they also want to see how you respond to it as a guide to what your reaction would be under the pressures of the job you seek. They will be influenced by the degree of poise you display, the personal traits you show and the manner in which you respond.

ABOUT THIS BOOK

This book contains tests divided into Examination Sections. Go through each test, answering every question in the margin. We have also attached a sample answer sheet at the back of the book that can be removed and used. At the end of each test look at the answer key and check your answers. On the ones you got wrong, look at the right answer choice and learn. Do not fill in the answers first. Do not memorize the questions and answers, but understand the answer and principles involved. On your test, the questions will likely be different from the samples. Questions are changed and new ones added. If you understand these past questions you should have success with any changes that arise. Tests may consist of several types of questions. We have additional books on each subject should more study be advisable or necessary for you. Finally, the more you study, the better prepared you will be. This book is intended to be the last thing you study before you walk into the examination room. Prior study of relevant texts is also recommended. NLC publishes some of these in our Fundamental Series. Knowledge and good sense are important factors in passing your exam. Good luck also helps. So now study this Passbook, absorb the material contained within and take that knowledge into the examination. Then do your best to pass that exam.

EXAMINATION SECTION

EXAMINATION SECTION
TEST 1

DIRECTIONS: Each question or incomplete statement is followed by several suggested answers or completions. Select the one that BEST answers the question or completes the statement. *PRINT THE LETTER OF THE CORRECT ANSWER IN THE SPACE AT THE RIGHT.*

1. The detection of counterfeiting and the apprehension of counterfeiters Is PRIMARILY the responsibility of the 1.____

    A. Federal Bureau of Investigation
    B. United States Secret Service
    C. Federal Reserve Board
    D. National Security Council

2. The term *legal tender* applies to 2.____

    A. a check, legally endorsed, and intended for deposit only
    B. money which may lawfully be used in the payment of debts
    C. foreign money whose rate of exchange is set by law
    D. uncoined gold or silver in the form of bullion bars

Questions 3-4.

DIRECTIONS: Questions 3 and 4 are to be answered SOLELY on the basis of the information contained in the following statement:

When a design for a new bank note of the Federal Government has been prepared by the Bureau of Engraving and Printing and has been approved by the Secretary of the Treasury, the engravers begin the work of cutting the design in steel. No one engraver does all the work. Each man is a specialist. One works only on portraits, another on lettering, another on scroll work, and so on. Each engraver, with a steel tool known as a graver, and aided by a powerful magnifying glass, carefully carves his portion of the design into the steel. He knows that one false cut or a slip of his tool, or one miscalculation of width or depth of line, may destroy the merit of his work. A single mistake means that months or weeks of labor will have been in vain. The Bureau is proud of the fact that no counterfeiter ever has duplicated the excellent work of its expert engravers.

3. According to the above statement, each engraver in the Bureau of Engraving and Printing 3.____

    A. must be approved by the Secretary of the Treasury before he can begin work on the design for a new bank note
    B. is responsible for engraving a complete design of a new bank note himself
    C. designs new bank notes and submits them for approval to the Secretary of the Treasury
    D. performs only a specific part of the work of engraving a design for a new bank note

4. According to the above statement, 4.____

A. an engraver's tools are not available to a counterfeiter
B. mistakes made in engraving a design can be corrected immediately with little delay in the work of the Bureau
C. the skilled work of the engravers has not been successfully reproduced by counterfeiters
D. careful carving and cutting by the engravers is essential to prevent damage to equipment

5. The public lays down the rules governing the type of service that it expects to be given. These rules are expressed partly in laws and partly in public opinion, which at any time may be made into law. Private business and government departments have, and always have had, the task of giving the public what it expects, a task which has lately come to be called public relations. According to the above statement,

    A. government departments have the task of serving the public as it wishes to be served
    B. private firms emphasize public relations more than public agencies do
    C. the rules for giving the public the service it expects are all eventually made into laws
    D. the task of public relations is to inform the public about the work of government departments

6. Certain personal qualities are required of an employee who is to perform a particular assignment efficiently. Since each employee possesses different qualities, experience indicates that it is important to seek and select the employee who possesses the personal qualities required for the particular assignment.
According to the above statement,

    A. the personal qualities of an employee should be changed to fit a particular assignment
    B. personal qualities are more important than experience in the performance of an assignment
    C. an assignment should be changed to fit the personal qualities of the employee assigned to it
    D. the employee selected for an assignment should have the personal qualities needed to perform it

7. A cashier has to make many arithmetic calculations in connection with his work. Skill in arithmetic comes readily with practice; no special talent is needed.
On the basis of the above statement, it is MOST accurate to state that

    A. the most important part of a cashier's job is to make calculations
    B. few cashiers have the special ability needed to handle arithmetic problems easily
    C. without special talent, cashiers cannot learn to do the calculations they are required to do in their work
    D. a cashier can, with practice, learn to handle the computations he is required to make

8. A bonded employee is much less likely to be tempted to steal money than an unbonded one, for he knows that a bonding company will prosecute him for the sake of principle, whereas an employer might not ordinarily take any action against an employee if there is no hope of recovering the stolen money.
   The MOST valid implication of the above statement is that

   A. a bonded employee if often tempted to steal because he knows that his employer is protected against the loss
   B. a bonding company will attempt to find and punish the guilty employee even when the stolen money cannot be recovered
   C. an employer whose bonded employees do not steal is wasting the money spent to bond them
   D. it is wasteful for a bonding company to prosecute an employee when there is no chance of recovering the stolen money

9. The BEST of the following attitudes regarding departmental rules and regulations for a cashier to take is that they

   A. are simply a means for justifying disciplinary action taken by a supervisor
   B. are to be interpreted by each employee as he sees fit
   C. must be obeyed even if they seem unreasonable in some cases
   D. should be read and studied but may be ignored whenever an employee feels it is necessary to do so

10. It is MOST important for a cashier who is assigned to perform a lengthy monotonous task to

    A. perform this task before doing his other work
    B. ask another cashier to assist him to dispose of the task quickly
    C. perform this task only when his other work has been completed
    D. take measures to prevent mistakes in performing this task

11. Although accuracy and speed are both important for a cashier in the performance of his work, accuracy should be considered more important MAINLY because

    A. most supervisors insist on accurate work
    B. much time is lost in correcting errors
    C. a rapid rate of work cannot be maintained for any length of time
    D. speedy workers are usually inaccurate

12. Of the following, the CHIEF reason why a cashier should not be late to work in the morning is that

    A. he will probably be penalized for his lateness
    B. the work of his unit may be delayed because of his tardiness
    C. he will set a bad example for the other employees to follow
    D. a poor attendance record may affect his supervisor's evaluation of his work

13. A cashier who handles large quantities of currency should know that the term *Silver Certificate* usually referred to

    A. a receipt for silver bars deposited with a bank
    B. a form of paper money that is acceptable only for the payment of non-business debts

C. a certificate issued by a refiner of silver metal to show the purity of his product
D. a form of paper money that is backed by silver owned by the United States Government

14. There are 12 consecutively numbered Federal Reserve Districts, each having as its symbol a number and the corresponding letter of the alphabet. The Federal Reserve Bank in each district has the same symbol as that of its district. For example, the Federal Reserve Bank of Boston is in the first Federal Reserve District and has as its symbol the number *1* and the letter *A*. The other districts, in numerical order, are New York, Philadelphia, Cleveland, Richmond, Atlanta, Chicago, St. Louis, Minneapolis, Kansas City, Dallas, and San Francisco.
According to the above statement, the Federal Reserve Bank of Philadelphia is represented by the

A. number *2* and the letter *B*
B. number *2* and the letter *C*
C. number *3* and the letter *B*
D. number *3* and the letter *C*

15. Of the following, the MOST important reason for a cashier to know the portraits that appear on each denomination of paper currency is that

A. he will be able to count bills merely by looking at the portraits
B. familiarity with portraits may help him to identify a counterfeit bill that has had its denomination changed from a lower to a higher amount
C. a greater knowledge of currency may help increase his promotional opportunities
D. the United States Treasury Department sometimes changes the portraits appearing on various currency denominations

16. The one of the following which is a characteristic of a genuine bill is that its portrait

A. has a fine screen of regular lines in its background
B. has irregular and broken lines in its background
C. has a very dark blue background
D. merges into the background

17. Of the following characteristics, the one that is LEAST helpful in deciding whether a bill is counterfeit is that the

A. portrait is dull, smudgy or scratchy
B. serial numbers are unevenly spaced
C. geometric lathework is broken and indistinct
D. ink rubs off when the bill is rubbed on a piece of paper

18. The color of the Treasury seal and serial number on a United States Note is always

A. blue   B. gray   C. green   D. red

19. The saw teeth points on the rim of the Treasury seal on a genuine bill are generally

A. blunt and uneven   B. broken off and faded
C. indistinct   D. sharp and evenly spaced

20. If one-half of a mutilated genuine bill is sent to the Currency Redemption Division of the Treasury Department, the bill will

    A. be redeemed at one-half of its face value
    B. be redeemed at three-fifths of its face value
    C. be redeemed at its full face value
    D. not be redeemed at all

20._____

21. The color of the Treasury seal and serial number on a Federal Reserve Note is always

    A. blue   B. brown   C. green   D. red

21._____

22. The serial number on the face of a bill is printed

    A. to the right of the portrait and to the lower left of the portrait
    B. to the left of the portrait and to the lower right of the portrait
    C. directly above the portrait and directly below the portrait
    D. in the upper left corner and the lower left corner

22._____

23. The color of the check letter on the face of a bill is always

    A. black   B. blue   C. green   D. red

23._____

24. The face plate number on the face of a bill is printed in the

    A. upper left corner   B. upper right corner
    C. lower left corner   D. lower right corner

24._____

25. If three-fifths of a mutilated genuine bill is sent to the Currency Redemption Division of the Treasury Department, the bill will

    A. be redeemed at one-half of its face value
    B. be redeemed at three-fifths of its face value
    C. be redeemed at its full face value
    D. not be redeemed at all

25._____

Questions 26 - 35.

DIRECTIONS: In Column I below are listed the names of ten men and buildings. In Column II are listed seven paper currency denominations and a category *None of the above denominations.*

In questions 26 to 35, for each man or building in Column I, print in the correspondingly numbered space on your answer sheet, the capital letter preceding the denomination in Column II on which the man or building appears. If the man or building appears on none of the listed denominations, print the letter *H* in the correspondingly numbered space on your answer sheet.

COLUMN I		COLUMN II	
26.	Alexander Hamilton	A. $1	26. ___
27.	White House	B. $2	27. ___
28.	Benjamin Franklin	C. $5	28. ___
29.	Mount Vernon	D. $10	29. ___
30.	Thomas Jefferson	E. $20	30. ___
31.	U.S. Treasury Department	F. $50	31. ___
32.	Andrew Jackson	G. $100	32. ___
33.	United States Capitol	H. None of the above denominations	33. ___
34.	George Washington		34. ___
35.	Abraham Lincoln		35. ___

KEY (CORRECT ANSWERS)

1.	B	11.	B	21.	C	31.	D
2.	B	12.	B	22.	A	32.	E
3.	D	13.	D	23.	A	33.	F
4.	C	14.	D	24.	D	34.	A
5.	A	15.	B	25.	C	35.	C
6.	D	16.	A	26.	D		
7.	D	17.	D	27.	E		
8.	B	18.	D	28.	G		
9.	C	19.	D	29.	H		
10.	D	20.	A	30.	B		

TEST 2

DIRECTIONS: Each question or incomplete statement is followed by several suggested answers or completions. Select the one that BEST answers the question or completes the statement. *PRINT THE LETTER OF THE CORRECT ANSWER IN THE SPACE AT THE RIGHT.*

1. Of the following, the characteristic which describes a genuine coin MOST accurately is that the coin usually

   A. can be bent easily at the edges
   B. can be cut easily with a knife
   C. has a bell-like ring when dropped on a hard surface
   D. will not bounce when dropped on a hard surface

   1.____

2. The corrugations on the outer edge of a genuine coin are usually

   A. even and regular
   B. indistinct and blackened
   C. the same as on a counterfeit coin
   D. uneven and crooked

   2.____

3. When comparing counterfeit coins with genuine ones, most counterfeit coins usually feel

   A. greasy   B. cold   C. sticky   D. damp

   3.____

4. A cashier who, in the course of his duties, suffers even a minor cut should have it properly cared for so that there will be no chance for infection to set in. Amputations, and even deaths, have resulted from small neglected wounds. According to the above statement, it is MOST accurate to state that

   A. a minor cut is not usually a cause for concern
   B. minor injuries are usually worse than they seem to be
   C. minor injuries should not be neglected
   D. small wounds are more dangerous than big ones

   4.____

5. Certain types of money may be photographed only with the permission of the Secretary of the Treasury. His permission is not required to photograph

   A. bills   B. bonds, bills and coins
   C. coins   D. either coins or bills

   5.____

6. Sometimes in the performance of his duties, a cashier must act alone, without advice from his superior and without reference to any books or other authority for guidance. According to this statement, a cashier must, in the exercise of his duties, sometimes display

   A. sincerity   B. caution
   C. initiative   D. courtesy

   6.____

7. To say that a cashier is METICULOUS in the performance of his duties is to say that he is

   A. extremely careful   B. highly enthusiastic
   C. unusually fast   D. prone to error

   7.____

8. The word NEGOTIABLE as used in business transactions means MOST NEARLY

   A. valueless
   B. transferable
   C. expensive
   D. profitable

9. An order which is RESCINDED is

   A. cancelled
   B. adopted
   C. clarified
   D. misunderstood

10. The word REMUNERATION means MOST NEARLY

    A. responsibility
    B. compensation
    C. complexity
    D. promotional opportunity

11. Assume that you are a cashier in an agency. Of the following, the MOST important reason why you should be courteous and tactful in dealing with visitors to your agency is that

    A. some of the visitors may show their appreciation of your courtesy by writing to your supervisor commending your work
    B. visitors who are treated courteously will probably treat you in the same manner
    C. visitors who are treated discourteously may ask your superior to take disciplinary action against you
    D. it is your responsibility to give the visitors a favorable impression of the agency

12. Assume that, as a cashier, you have been assigned the task of training a new employee in the work of collecting payments from the public.
    Of the following, the MOST effective technique to follow in training this employee is for you to

    A. encourage him by praising the work he has done correctly, but do not show him the mistakes he has made
    B. insist that he obey your instructions completely even if your instructions may not be clear to him
    C. encourage him to ask questions if he does not understand any of the work
    D. give him a complete understanding of his job by showing him the incorrect, as well as the correct ways of doing his work

13. Subtract the total of 9 quarters, 17 dimes and 12 nickels from the total of 6 half-dollars, 14 quarters, 8 dimes and 6 nickels.
    The *answer* is

    A. $2.05   B. $3.05   C. $3.15   D. $4.15

14. A certified check is one that

    A. states the purpose for which it is drawn
    B. has funds set aside to cover it by the bank upon which it is drawn
    C. is written by the bank upon which it is drawn
    D. requires the endorsements of both the payee and the maker before it can be cashed

15. Of the following, the MOST accurate description of a cashier's check is that it

    A. can be cashed only by the cashier of the Bank upon which it is drawn
    B. is drawn by a bank in payment for the services of one of its cashiers
    C. is drawn payable to the cashier of a bank by a depositor of the bank
    D. is drawn by a bank on its own funds and signed by its cashier

16. If, on a check, the amount payable expressed in words and the amount payable expressed in figures are not the same, then the amount payable is the

    A. amount in figures
    B. amount in words
    C. average of the two amounts
    D. lesser of the two amounts

Questions 17 - 20.

DIRECTIONS: Column I lists four different endorsements that a man named John Doe uses to endorse checks. Column II lists the names of five types of endorsements. In questions 17 to 20, for each endorsement listed in Column I, select the correct name in Column II by which that endorsement is generally known.

On your answer sheet, next to the number corresponding to each type of endorsement listed in Column I, write the capital letter preceding the name listed in Column II by which that endorsement is generally known.

COLUMN I

17. John Doe
18. Without recourse John Doe
19. Pay to the order of Richard Roe John Doe
20. Pay to the order of City Bank for deposit only John Doe

COLUMN II

A. blank
B. full
C. qualified
D. conditional
E. restricted

Questions 21 - 25.

DIRECTIONS: Questions 21 to 25 are based on the following table.

COLLECTIONS BY CASHIERS FOR ONE WEEK

Name of Cashier	Monday	Tuesday	Wednesday	Thursday	Friday
Adams	$7487	$7435	$8864	$9264	$9876
Baker	9687	8643	8198	7415	8714
Taylor	7403	'6035	9722	9683	9512
Moore	6869	8212	9417	8933	9463
Foster	9129	9069	7734	8121	9596

21. Of the following, the day of the week on which the MOST money was collected is

    A. Tuesday   B. Wednesday
    C. Thursday   D. Friday

22. Of the following, the day of the week on which the LEAST money was collected is   22.____

    A. Monday   B. Tuesday
    C. Wednesday   D. Friday

23. The average amount collected per day by all the cashiers is   23.____

    A. less than $42,000
    B. between $42,000 and $42,500
    C. between $42,501 and $43,000
    D. more than $43,000

24. Foster's total collection for Monday, Tuesday and Friday are greater than Taylor's total collections for the same three days by MOST NEARLY   24.____

    A. 12%   B. 17%   C. 21%   D. 83%

25. The average amount collected per cashier on Wednesday   25.____

    A. was less than the average amount collected per cashier on Monday by $328
    B. was greater than the average amount collected per cashier on Monday by $672
    C. was less than the average amount collected per cashier on Thursday by $104
    D. was greater than the average amount collected per cashier on Thursday by $886

26. A bag contains 800 coins. Of these, 10 per cent are dimes, 30 per cent are nickels, and the rest are quarters.
    The amount of money in the bag is   26.____

    A. less than $150   B. between $150 and $300
    C. between $301 and $450   D. more than $450

27. On March 1, the revenue division of a city department counted $800,000. The money counted on March 2 was 10 per cent less than the money counted on March 1. If the money counted on March 3 was 10 per cent greater than the money counted on March 2, then the money counted on March 3 was   27.____

    A. $802,000   B. $792,000
    C. $720,000   D. $700,000

28. If one cashier can count a certain sum of money in 2 hours, and another cashier can count the same sum in 3 hours, then both cashiers working together can count this sum in   28.____

    A. 50 minutes   B. 1 hour and 10 minutes
    C. 1 hour and 12 minutes   D. 1 hour and 20 minutes

29. If the real estate tax is $4.11 per $100 of assessed valuation, the tax on real estate assessed at $19,500 is MOST NEARLY   29.____

    A. $47   B. $650   C. $800   D. $900

30. The tax collections in a tax office for the week ending January 11th were $468,693.80. If this amount was 20 per cent greater than the tax collections for the week ending January 4th, the tax collections for the week ending January 4th were MOST NEARLY   30.____

    A. $328,090   B. $375,000   C. $390,580   D. $393,705

31. Assume that the real estate tax rate is $4.08 per $100 of assessed valuation. If the tax on a house is $1,040.40, then the assessed valuation of the house is

    A. $25,500
    B. $24,000
    C. $27,000
    D. $28,500

32. Cashier X receives payments from 6 taxpayers every 15 minutes. Cashier Y receives payments from 15 taxpayers every half-hour. If Cashier X begins work at 9 a.m., and Cashier Y begins work at 9:30 a.m., the time at which the two Cashiers will have received payments from an equal number of taxpayers is

    A. 11 a.m.
    B. 11:30 a.m.
    C. 12 noon
    D. 12:30 p.m.

33. The real estate tax on a piece of real property in a certain city is $1,082.40. If the assessed valuation of the property is $26,400, then the tax rate per $100 of assessed valuation is

    A. less than $4.05
    B. between $4.05 and $4.08
    C. between $4.09 and $4.14
    D. more than $4.14

34. If $300 is invested at simple interest so as to yield a return of $18 in 9 months, the amount of money that must be invested at the same rate of interest so as to yield a return of $120 in 6 months is

    A. $3000
    B. $3300
    C. $2000
    D. $2300

35. Mr. Smith is reconciling his bank balance on November 15th by the use of the following information:
    Balance as per Bank Statement, October 31st - $15,932.20 Total Checks Outstanding, October 31st - 1,642.29 Total Deposits, November 1st to November 15th - 715.00 Total Checks Drawn, November 1st to November
    15th -   1,329.63
    According to the above information, the balance that Mr. Smith's checkbook should show as of the close of business on November 15th is MOST NEARLY

    A. $18,290
    B. $16,647
    C. $13,675
    D. $12,960

KEY (CORRECT ANSWERS)

1. C	11. D	21. D	31. A
2. A	12. C	22. B	32. B
3. A	13. B	23. C	33. C
4. C	14. B	24. C	34. A
5. C	15. D	25. B	35. C
6. C	16. B	26. A	
7. A	17. A	27. B	
8. B	18. C	28. C	
9. A	19. B	29. C	
10. B	20. E	30. C	

———

EXAMINATION SECTION
TEST 1

DIRECTIONS: Each question or incomplete statement is followed by several suggested answers or completions. Select the one that BEST answers the question or completes the statement. *PRINT THE LETTER OF THE CORRECT ANSWER IN THE SPACE AT THE RIGHT.*

Questions 1-7.

DIRECTIONS: Questions 1 through 7 are to be answered on the basis of the following income statement.

Laura Lee's Bridal Shop
Income Statement
For the Year Ended December 31, 2018

Revenue:		
New & Used Bridal Gowns & Accessories		$55,000
Expenses:		
Advertisement Expense	$ 2,000	
Salaries Expense	12,000	
Dry cleaning & Alterations	10,000	
Utilities	1,500	
Total Expenses		25,500
Net Income		$29,500

1. What is the period of time covered by this income statement?   1._____

    A. January-December 2017
    B. December 2018
    C. January 2017-December 2018
    D. January-December 2018

2. What is the source of the revenue?   2._____

    A. New and used bridal gowns, advertisements, salaries, dry cleaning, and utilities
    B. Advertisements, salaries, dry cleaning, alterations, and utilities
    C. New and used bridal gowns and accessories
    D. Net income

3. What is the total revenue?   3._____

    A. $25,500   B. $55,000   C. $29,500   D. $79,500

4. Which of the following are expenses?   4._____

    A. Salaries
    B. New and used bridal gowns and accessories
    C. Revenue
    D. New and used bridal gowns, advertisements, and dry cleaning

5. What are the total expenses?   5._____

    A. $55,000   B. $29,500   C. $79,500   D. $25,500

6. There is a resulting net income because

   A. total revenue and total expenses are combined
   B. net income is greater than total revenue
   C. the total revenue is greater than total expenses
   D. the total revenue is less than total expenses

7. Is this statement an interim statement?

   A. Yes, because it covers an entire accounting period
   B. No, because it covers an entire accounting period
   C. Yes, because it covers a period of less than a year
   D. No, because it covers a period of more than a year

8. What is the name of the accounting report that may show either a net profit or a net loss for an accounting period?

   A. Income statement
   B. Balance sheet
   C. Statement of capital
   D. Classified balance sheet

9. What are the two main parts of the body of the income statement?

   A. Cash and Capital
   B. Revenue and Expenses
   C. Liabilities and Capital
   D. Assets and Notes Payable

10. If total revenue exceeds total expenses for an accounting period, what is the difference called?

    A. Gross income
    B. Total liabilities
    C. Total assets
    D. Net income

11. In the body of a balance sheet, what are the three sections called?

    A. Assets and liabilities
    B. Cash, liabilities, and revenue
    C. Assets, liabilities, and capital
    D. Revenue, assets, and capital

12. What business record shows the results of the proprietor's borrowing assets from the business, usually in anticipation of profits?

    A. Proprietor's withdrawals
    B. Accounts payable
    C. Liabilities and Capital
    D. Total liabilities

Questions 13-24.

DIRECTIONS: For each transaction given for Mona's Magic Moments Hair Salon in Questions 13 through 24, identify which journal the transaction should be recorded in.

13. April 1: Mona, the owner, paid the month's rent - $600.00; check no. 356.

    A. General
    B. Cash disbursements
    C. Purchases
    D. Sales

14. April 6: the salon purchased $300.00 worth of styling products on account from Pomme de Terre Company.   14._____

    A. Cash disbursements   B. General
    C. Sales   D. Purchases

15. April 8: sold $100.00 worth of hair products on account to Mrs. Angela Bray.   15._____

    A. Sales   B. Purchases
    C. Cash disbursements   D. General

16. April 11: the owner, Mona Ramen, withdrew $80.00 of styling products for personal use.   16._____

    A. Sales   B. Cash receipts
    C. General   D. Cash disbursements

17. April 13: paid Pomme de Terre Company $300.00 on account; check 357.   17._____

    A. Purchases   B. Cash disbursements
    C. Cash receipts   D. General

18. April 15: cash sales to date were $4,607.00.   18._____

    A. Cash disbursements   B. Purchases
    C. Sales   D. General

19. April 17: issued credit slip #17 to Mrs. Angela Bray for $25.00 for merchandise returned.   19._____

    A. Cash disbursements   B. Cash receipts
    C. Sales   D. General

20. April 19: paid electric bill for $250.00; check no. 358.   20._____

    A. Cash disbursements   B. Purchases
    C. General   D. Cash receipts

21. April 21: received $75.00 from Mrs. Angela Bray for balance due on account.   21._____

    A. Sales   B. Cash disbursements
    C. Cash receipts   D. Purchases

22. April 23: sold $88.00 of hair products on account to Ms. Tania Alioto.   22._____

    A. Purchases   B. Sales
    C. Cash disbursements   D. Cash receipts

23. April 27: purchased $500.00 of equipment from Salon Stylings Merchandisers on account.   23._____

    A. Cash disbursements   B. Sales
    C. General   D. Purchases

24. April 30: cash sales to date were $5023.00.   24._____

    A. Purchases   B. Sales
    C. Cash receipts   D. General

Questions 25-30.

DIRECTIONS: Questions 25 through 30 are to be answered on the basis of the following ledger for a barbecue take-out restaurant owned and operated by Ruby Joiner.

25. What is the balance on the Cash account shown above? 25.____
    A. 2,012.00   B. 1,110.00   C. 3,122.00   D. 902.00

26. What is the balance on the Accounts receivable account shown above? 26.____
    A. 425.00   B. 875.00   C. 450.00   D. 1315.00

27. What is the balance on the Accounts payable account shown above? 27.____
    A. 1100.00   B. 1075.00   C. 25.00   D. 1125.00

28. Which of the above accounts has a balance of 1100.00? 28.____
    A. Accounts payable   B. Delivery Income
    C. Cash   D. Delivery equipment

29. Which of the above accounts has a balance of 12,000.00? 29.____
    A. Ruby Joiner, Capital
    B. Cash and Accounts receivable combined
    C. Delivery equipment
    D. None of the accounts

30. If you made a balance sheet out of the information listed above, Ruby Joiner's total assets would be 30.____
    A. 14,472.00   B. 12,297.00   C. 13,392.00   D. 13,487.00

Questions 31-34.

DIRECTIONS: Questions 31 through 34 are to be answered on the basis of the following information, to be included on a checking deposit ticket.

Five $20 bills; 11 $10 bills; 6 $5 bills; 47 $1 bills; 200 half dollars; 120 quarters; 112 dimes; 320 nickels; 67 pennies. Second National Bank (73-124) check of 152.34; Bank of the Midwest (13-298) check of 68.37; Great National Bank (32-165) check of 185.06.

31. What is the TOTAL currency for this deposit? 31.____
   A. $387   B. $287   C. $444.87   D. $157.87

32. What is the TOTAL coin for this deposit? 32.____
   A. $387   B. $287   C. $444.87   D. $157.87

33. What is the check total for this deposit? 33.____
   A. $692.77   B. $406   C. $405.77   D. $850.64

34. What is the TOTAL deposit? 34.____
   A. $444.87   B. $692.77   C. $851   D. $850.64

Questions 35-37.

DIRECTIONS: Questions 35 through 37 are to be answered on the basis of the following petty cash journal.

Date	Receipt No.	To Whom Paid	For What	Acct.#	Amount
10/2	1	Anna Jones - Mail	Postage	548	13.50
10/2	2	Jim Collins	Messenger	525	5.75
10/4	3	Anna Jones - Mail	Postage	548	13.50
10/5	4	Lucky Stores	Coffee	515	7.34
10/6	5	Tom Allen	Lunch w/customer	525	11.38

35. What is the TOTAL disbursement from this fund for the time period 10/1 through 10/6? 35.____
   A. $51.47   B. $40.09   C. $61.47   D. $26.59

36. How much money was disbursed to Account #548 during the time period 10/1-10/16? 36.____
   A. $51.47   B. $26   C. $27   D. $34.34

37. If the fund began the month with a total of $100.00, what amount was left in the fund at the end of business on 10/5? 37.____
   A. $48.53   B. $59.91   C. $51.47   D. $40.09

Questions 38-40.

DIRECTIONS: Questions 38 through 40 are to be answered on the basis of the following information.

A promissory note dated December 1, 2018, bearing interest at a rate of 12% and due in 90 days, is sent to a creditor. The face value of the note is $900.

38. What is the due date of the promissory note? 38._____
    A. January 15, 2019   B. March 1, 2019
    C. February 1, 2019   D. December 31, 2018

39. What is the TOTAL interest that will be earned on the note? 39._____
    A. $27   B. $270   C. $108   D. $10.80

40. What interest will be earned on the note for the old accounting period (December 1-31)? 40._____
    A. $90   B. $36   C. $9   D. $3.60

KEY (CORRECT ANSWERS)

1. D	11. C	21. C	31. B
2. C	12. A	22. B	32. D
3. B	13. B	23. D	33. C
4. A	14. D	24. B	34. D
5. D	15. A	25. D	35. A
6. C	16. C	26. A	36. C
7. B	17. B	27. B	37. B
8. A	18. C	28. B	38. B
9. B	19. D	29. C	39. A
10. D	20. A	30. D	40. C

TEST 2

DIRECTIONS: Each question or incomplete statement is followed by several suggested answers or completions. Select the one that BEST answers the question or completes the statement. *PRINT THE LETTER OF THE CORRECT ANSWER IN THE SPACE AT THE RIGHT.*

Questions 1-4.

DIRECTIONS: Questions 1 through 4 are to be answered on the basis of the following information, to be included in a deposit slip.

    14 twenty dollar bills   63 quarters
    52 ten dollar bills   22 dimes
    12 five dollar bills   44 nickels
    43 one dollar bills   70 pennies

Checks: $236.34 and $129.72

1. What is the TOTAL amount of currency for this deposit? 1.____
   A. $923.85   B. $1269.06   C. $903.00   D. $1299.91

2. What is the TOTAL amount of coin for this deposit? 2.____
   A. $20.85   B. $923.85   C. $903.00   D. $1299.91

3. What is the TOTAL amount of check for this deposit? 3.____
   A. $20.85   B. $366.06   C. $1299.91   D. $903.00

4. What is the TOTAL deposit for this slip? 4.____
   A. $1269.06   B. $903.00   C. $923.85   D. $1289.91

Questions 5-7.

DIRECTIONS: Questions 5 through 7 are to be answered on the basis of the following information.

Angela Martinez's last check stub balance was $675.50. Her bank statement balance dated April 30 was $652.00. A $250 deposit was in transit on that date. Outstanding checks were as follows: No. 127, $65.00; No. 129, $203.50; No. 130, $50.00. The bank service charge for the month was $5.00.

5. What was Angela Martinez's available checkbook balance on April 30? 5.____
   A. $652.00   B. $338.50   C. $583.50   D. $675.50

6. In order to reconcile her checkbook balance with her bank statement balance, what must Angela Martinez do? 6.____
   A. Add her checkbook balance to the balance on her bank statement
   B. Subtract her checkbook balance from the balance on her bank statement

19

C. Ignore her checkbook balance and adopt the balance on her bank statement
D. Adjust the checkbook balance by adding deposits and debiting outstanding checks and charges

7. The check stub balance referred to in the problem refers to the   7._____

   A. last check Angela Martinez recorded in her checkbook
   B. amount of money left in Angela Martinez's account according to her own calculations based on the checks, charges, and deposits she has written and recorded
   C. amount of money left in Angela Martinez's account according to the bank's calculations based on the checks, charges, and deposits posted to her account
   D. number of checks left in her checkbook

Questions 8-9.

DIRECTIONS: Questions 8 and 9 are to be answered on the basis of the following information.

Tu Nguyen, an interior designer, received his June bank statement on July 2. The balance was $622.66. His last check stub balance was $700. On comparing the two, he noticed that a deposit of $275 made on June 30 was not included on the statement; also, a bank service charge of $4 was deducted. Outstanding checks were as follows: No. 331, $97.50; No. 332, $207; No. 335, $25.40; and No. 336, $68.97.

8. What is Nguyen's CORRECT available bank balance?   8._____

   A. $494.79   B. $897.66   C. $700.00   D. $219.79

9. The bank statement balance referred to in the problem refers to the   9._____

   A. last check Tu Nguyen recorded in his checkbook
   B. last check presented for payment to Tu Nguyen's account
   C. amount of money left in Tu Nguyen's account according to the bank's calculations based on the checks, charges, and deposits posted to his account
   D. amount of money left in Tu Nguyen's account based on his own calculations of the checks, charges, and deposits he has written and recorded

10. What of the following endorsements would be an example of a simple Endorsement in Blank?   10._____

    A. Pay to the Order of Joanie Anderson
    B. Joanie Anderson
    C. For deposit only; Acct. No. 12345; Joanie Anderson
    D. Without Recourse; Joanie Anderson

11. Which of the following endorsements would limit the further purpose or use of the endorsed check?   11._____

    A. Pay to the Order of Joanie Anderson
    B. Joanie Anderson
    C. For deposit only; Acct. No. 12345; Joanie Anderson,
    D. Without Recourse; Joanie Anderson

12. Which of the following endorsements would protect the endorser from legal responsibility for payment, should the drawer have insufficient funds to honor his/her own check?

    A. Pay to the Order of Joanie Anderson
    B. Joanie Anderson
    C. For deposit only; Acct. No. 12345; Joanie Anderson
    D. Without Recourse; Joanie Anderson

Questions 13-24.

DIRECTIONS: Questions 13 - 24 are to be answered on the basis of the following ledger accounts for Wheelsmith Organic Farms.

Wheelsmith Organic Farms
Ledger Accounts

Cash	Accounts Payable	Service Supplies
Jan. 1 4,000	Jan. 1 2,000	Jan. 1 2,000

Shelley Wheelsmith, Capital	Machinery
Jan. 1 11,000	Jan. 1 7,000

13. Transaction #1: On January 5, Shelley Wheelsmith, the proprietor, received cash amounting to $5,000 as a result of returning machinery that had recently been purchased. What account(s) should this transaction be posted to?

    A. Cash
    B. Cash and Machinery
    C. Machinery
    D. Cash, Machinery, and Service Supplies

14. Transaction #2: On January 8, Shelley Wheelsmith, the proprietor, sent out a check for $600 in partial payment of the accounts payable.
    What account(s) should this transaction be posted to?

    A. Accounts Payable
    B. Accounts Payable and Cash
    C. Accounts Payable and Capital
    D. Cash

15. Transaction #3: On January 14, Shelley Wheelsmith, proprietor, made an additional investment in the business by contributing machinery valued at $1,500.
    What account(s) should this transaction be posted to?

    A. Machinery   B. Machinery and Capital
    C. Capital   D. Machinery and Cash

16. Transaction #4: On January 26, Shelley Wheelsmith, proprietor, purchased additional service supplies for $200. She agreed to pay the obligation in 30 days. What account(s) should this transaction be posted to?

A. Accounts Payable and Liabilities
B. Service supplies
C. Accounts Payable
D. Accounts Payable and Service supplies

17. Transaction #5: On January 31, Shelley Wheelsmith, proprietor, purchased service supplies paying cash of $50. What account(s) should this transaction be posted to? 17.____

   A. Service supplies
   B. Service supplies and Accounts Payable
   C. Cash and Service supplies
   D. Cash

18. What is the balance in the Cash account after all of these transactions are posted? 18.____

   A. $9,000   B. $1,000   C. $5,000   D. $8,350

19. What is the balance in the Machinery account after all of these transactions are posted? 19.____

   A. $7,000   B. $5,000   C. $3,500   D. $13,500

20. What is the balance in the Accounts Payable account after all of these transactions are posted? 20.____

   A. $800   B. $600   C. $2,600   D. $1,600

21. What is the balance in the Capital account after all of these transactions are posted? 21.____

   A. $12,500   B. $800   C. $11,600   D. $10,400

22. What is the balance in the Service supplies account after all of these transactions are posted? 22.____

   A. $2,000   B. $2,250   C. $750   D. $2,200

23. What are the total assets of Wheelsmith Organic Farms after these transactions have been posted? 23.____

   A. $10,600   B. $11,850   C. $14,100   D. $10,750

24. What are the total liabilities and capital for Wheelsmith Organic Farms after these transactions have been posted? 24.____

   A. $14,100   B. $12,500   C. $11,850   D. $10,600

Questions 25-28.

DIRECTIONS: Questions 25 through 28 are to be answered on the basis of the following information.

At the end of an accounting period, Andy's Framing Gallery recorded the following information: Sales, $125,225; Merchandise Inventory, December 31, $95,325; Purchases Returns and Allowances, $3,500; Merchandise Inventory, January 1, $98,725; Freight on Purchases, $2,500; Purchases, $120,000.

25. What are the net purchases for Andy's Framing Gallery during the accounting period? 25.____
    A. $120,000   B. $119,000   C. $3,500   D. $122,500

26. What is the cost of goods available for sale? 26.____
    A. $119,000   B. $98,725   C. $95,325   D. $217,725

27. What is the total cost of goods sold for this accounting period? 27.____
    A. $217,725   B. $95,325   C. $122,400   D. $125,225

28. What is the gross profit on sales for this accounting period? 28.____
    A. $2825   B. $2500   C. $125,225   D. $122,400

Questions 29-40.

DIRECTIONS: Questions 29 through 40 are to be answered on the basis of the following information.

The Joie de Vivre Co. received the promissory notes listed below during the last quarter of its calendar year:

	Date	Face Amount	Terms	Interest Rate	Date Discounted	Discount Rate
(1)	10/8	$3,600	30 days	-	10/18	9%
(2)	9/22	$8,000	60 days	6%	10/1	7%
(3)	11/15	$3,000	90 days	7%	11/20	8%

29. What is the due date for the first note? 29.____
    A. 12/31   B. 11/7   C. 12/7   D. 10/31

30. What interest will be due when the first note matures? 30.____
    A. $3   B. $3,600   C. $30   D. $0

31. What is the maturity value of the first note? 31.____
    A. $3,600   B. $3,630   C. $0   D. $3,603

32. What is the discount period for the first note? 32.____
    A. One fiscal year   B. 10 days
    C. 20 days   D. One month

33. What is the due date for the second note? 33.____
    A. 12/21   B. 11/21   C. 10/21   D. 1/21

34. What interest will be due when the second note matures? 34.____
    A. $60   B. $800.00   C. $8.00   D. $80.00

35. What is the maturity value of the second note? 35.____
    A. $8,000   B. $8,080   C. $8,800   D. $8,008

36. What is the discount period for the second note?

    A. 51 days   B. 10 days   C. 360 days   D. 60 days

37. What is the due date for the third note?

    A. 1/14   B. 12/15   C. 12/31   D. 2/13

38. What interest will be due when the third note matures?

    A. $5.25   B. $52.50   C. $525   D. $90

39. What is the maturity value of the third note?

    A. $3525   B. $3005.25   C. $3052.50   D. $3090

40. What is the discount period for the third note?

    A. 60 days   B. 85 days   C. 5 days   D. 90 days

KEY (CORRECT ANSWERS)

1. C	11. C	21. A	31. A
2. A	12. D	22. B	32. C
3. B	13. B	23. C	33. B
4. D	14. B	24. A	34. D
5. C	15. B	25. B	35. B
6. D	16. D	26. D	36. A
7. B	17. C	27. C	37. D
8. A	18. D	28. A	38. B
9. C	19. C	29. B	39. C
10. B	20. D	30. D	40. B

TEST 3

DIRECTIONS: Each question or incomplete statement is followed by several suggested answers or completions. Select the one that BEST answers the question or completes the statement. *PRINT THE LETTER OF THE CORRECT ANSWER IN THE SPACE AT THE RIGHT.*

Questions 1-8.

DIRECTIONS: Questions 1 through 8 are to be answered on the basis of the following Balance Sheet.

Laura Lee's Bridal Shop
Balance Sheet
December 31, 2018

Assets

Cash	$14,000	
Accounts Receivable	3,000	
Bridal Accessories	10,000	
Gowns and Other Inventory	30,000	
Total Assets		$57,000

Liabilities and Capital

Accounts Payable	$ 4,000	
Notes Payable	28,000	
Total Liabilities		$32,000
Laura Lee, Capital		25,000
Total Liabilities and Capital		$57,000

1. When was the balance sheet prepared?

    A. January 2019
    B. December 31, 2018
    C. After the close of the 2018 fiscal year
    D. December 1, 2018

2. How does the date on this balance sheet differ from the date on the statement of capital or income statement?

    A. It doesn't differ. The dates for each statement signify the same time period.
    B. The date on a balance sheet represents the period during which any changes indicated on the statement took place, whereas the other financial statements represent the moment in time when the statement was prepared.
    C. The date on a balance sheet represents the moment in time when the statement was prepared, whereas the other financial statements represent the period during which any changes indicated on the statement took place.
    D. The date on a balance sheet indicates an entire year, whereas the dates on the other statements indicate a single month.

3. Can Laura Lee purchase more bridal gowns for the business paying cash of $16,000?

    A. *No*, because the business has only $14,000 cash available
    B. *Yes*, because the business has $57,000 cash available
    C. *Yes*, because the business has $57,000 available in assets
    D. *No*, because the business has $57,000 in liabilities

4. What is the owner's equity of Laura Lee's Bridal Shop?
   Since total equity consists of total _____, total equity is _____.

   A. assets minus total liabilities and proprietor's capital; $0
   B. assets minus total liabilities; $25,000
   C. assets; $57,000
   D. liabilities and proprietor's capital; $57,000

5. What is the TOTAL amount of Laura Lee's claim against the total assets of the business?

   A. $57,000   B. $25,000   C. $0   D. $39,000

6. What is the amount of the creditors' claims against the assets of the business?

   A. $4,000   B. $57,000   C. $32,000   D. $28,000

7. What is the net income for the period?

   A. $57,000
   B. $0
   C. $25,000
   D. This information cannot be obtained from the balance sheet

8. What was the value of Laura Lee's ownership in this business on January 1, 2004?

   A. $25,000
   B. $57,000
   C. $14,000
   D. This information cannot be obtained from the balance sheet

Questions 9-21.

DIRECTIONS: Each of the transactions described in Questions 9 through 21 occurred within an accounting period. For each question, indicate which of the four journals the transaction would be recorded in.

9. Sale of goods on account

   A. Cash receipts   B. Cash payments
   C. General   D. Sales

10. Cash payment of a promissory note

    A. Cash payments   B. Cash receipts
    C. Sales   D. General

11. Received a credit memo from a creditor

    A. Purchases   B. General
    C. Sales   D. Cash payments

12. Sale of merchandise for cash

    A. Purchases   B. General
    C. Cash receipts   D. Cash payments

13. Received a check from a customer in partial payment of an oral agreement 13.____

    A. Purchases   B. Sales
    C. General   D. Cash receipts

14. Issued a credit memo to a customer 14.____

    A. Purchases   B. General
    C. Cash payments   D. Sales

15. Received a promissory note in place of an oral agreement from a customer 15.____

    A. General   B. Cash payments
    C. Cash receipts   D. Sales

16. Paid monthly rent 16.____

    A. General   B. Purchases
    C. Cash payments   D. Cash receipts

17. Sale of a service on credit 17.____

    A. Cash receipts   B. General
    C. Purchases   D. Sales

18. Purchase of office furniture on credit 18.____

    A. General   B. Purchases
    C. Cash payments   D. Cash receipts

19. Purchased merchandise for cash 19.____

    A. Cash payments   B. Cash receipts
    C. Sales   D. General

20. Cash refund to a customer 20.____

    A. Cash receipts   B. Sales
    C. General   D. Cash payments

21. Purchases made on credit 21.____

    A. Purchases   B. Sales
    C. Cash receipts   D. General

Questions 22-26.

DIRECTIONS: Questions 22 through 26 are to be answered on the basis of the following inventory, purchased by International Soap and Candle Traders, Inc.

700 units at $4.50, 320 units at $3.75, 550 units at $2.75, and 475 units at $1.90

22. Calculate the total price of the units that cost $4.50. 22.____

    A. $315   B. $31,500   C. $3,150   D. $2,800

23. Calculate the total price of the units that cost $3.75. 23.____

    A. $2062.50   B. $12,000   C. $120   D. $1,200

24. Calculate the total price of the units that cost $2.75.

    A. $1,512.50   B. $15,125   C. $151.25   D. $550

25. Calculate the total price of the units that cost $1.90.

    A. $90.25   B. $9025   C. $902.50   D. $475

26. Calculate the average cost per unit.

    A. $27   B. $33.10   C. $0.30   D. $3.31

27. The interest on a promissory note is recorded at which of the following times?

    A. When the debt is incurred
    B. At the end of the accounting period
    C. When the note is paid
    D. At the beginning of each month

28. The interest on a promissory note begins accruing at which of the following times?

    A. When the debt is incurred
    B. At the end of the accounting period
    C. When the note is paid
    D. At the beginning of each month

29. The maturity value of an interest-bearing note is the

    A. interest accrued on the note plus a service charge imposed by the lender
    B. interest accrued on the note
    C. face value of the note
    D. principal of the note plus interest

30. A cash receipts journal is used to record the

    A. number of cash sales a business makes
    B. number of credit sales a business makes
    C. collection of cash made by the business
    D. expenditure of cash made by the business

31. Calculate the interest on a promissory note issued for $3,000 at an interest rate of 8%, due in 360 days. (Assume a banking year of 360 days.)

    A. $300   B. $240   C. $60   D. $360

32. Calculate the total payment due for a promissory note issued for $1,000 at an interest rate of 10%, due in 90 days. (Assume a banking year of 360 days.)

    A. $25   B. $1050   C. $1000   D. $1025

33. Calculate the total payment due for a promissory note issued for $5,000 at an interest rate of 6%, due in 60 days. (Assume a banking year of 360 days.)

    A. $5,050   B. $50   C. $5,000   D. $5,300

34. Calculate the interest on a promissory note issued for $1,700 at an interest rate of 12%, due in 45 days. (Assume a banking year of 360 days.) 34.____

    A. $204   B. $1725.50   C. $25.50   D. $1904

35. Calculate the interest on a promissory note issued for $600 at an interest rate of 9%, due in 90 days. (Assume a banking year of 360 days.) 35.____

    A. $13.50   B. $135   C. $54   D. $540

KEY (CORRECT ANSWERS)

1.	B	16.	C
2.	C	17.	D
3.	A	18.	B
4.	B	19.	A
5.	B	20.	D
6.	C	21.	A
7.	D	22.	C
8.	D	23.	D
9.	D	24.	A
10.	A	25.	C
11.	B	26.	D
12.	C	27.	C
13.	D	28.	A
14.	B	29.	D
15.	A	30.	C

31. B
32. D
33. A
34. C
35. A

EXAMINATION SECTION
TEST 1

DIRECTIONS: Each question or incomplete statement is followed by several suggested answers or completions. Select the one that BEST answers the question or completes the statement. *PRINT THE LETTER OF THE CORRECT ANSWER IN THE SPACE AT THE RIGHT.*

1. A woman in her mid-30s comes up to your desk and asks you how she can apply to work at your office. You do not know the immediate answer to that question.
   Which of the following would be the BEST way to respond to her request?
   A. Tell her what sounds like the right answer
   B. Tell her to talk to your boss and show her how to do that
   C. Explain you are not allowed to give out confidential information to the public
   D. Inform her that you do not know right now, but you will find out

2. A person approaches the customer service desk and asks you to do something that you are ultimately unable to do.
   Which of the following should you avoid doing next?
   A. Opening your policy handbook and reading from it verbatim
   B. Clarifying why you cannot do what he or she is asking of you
   C. Crafting detailed and precise statements
   D. Giving the person alternative options

3. When talking to someone from the public, which of the following statements would be LEAST frustrating for the customer to hear?
   A. "You'll have to…"   B. "Mr. X will be back at any moment…"
   C. "Let me see what I can do…"   D. "I'll do my best…"

4. Your office recently received a letter from an individual expressing extreme frustration and disappointment at how it was handling the customer's problems. You have written an apology letter and are reviewing it before sending it to the customer.
   You should ensure the letter is NOT
   A. sincere   B. official
   C. personal   D. sent immediately

5. If you are unable to provide a certain service or product with dependability and accuracy, it would be defined as a lack of
   A. courtesy   B. reliability   C. assurance   D. responsiveness

6. As most civil service employees know, customer feedback can be, and usually is, an integral part of customer service.
Which of the following feedback scenarios would be MOST useful to your organization?
   A. When it is an ongoing feedback system
   B. When centered on internal customers
   C. When it is focused on only a few indicators
   D. When every employee can see the feedback coming in

7. Which of the following is the LEAST important factor in making sure a customer survey is a valuable tool for your company?
   A. Taking every precaution to ensure the survey input is maintained in a confidential manner
   B. Making sure the customers believe in the confidentiality of the survey
   C. Ensuring confidentiality by having an outside company administer the survey
   D. Making sure the employees buy in and promote the survey to customers

8. Which of the following would NOT be considered part of the resolution process when identifying and dealing with a customers' problems?
   A. Following up with the customer after resolving the issue
   B. Listening and responding to each complaint the customer registers
   C. Giving the customer what they originally requested
   D. Promising the customer whatever you need to

9. A customer approaches you with a complaint. You want to arrive at a fair solution to the problem.
What is the FIRST step you should take in this situation?
   A. Immediately defend your company from any customer criticisms
   B. Listen to the customer describe their problem
   C. Ask the customer questions to confirm the type of problem they are having
   D. Determine a solution to the customer's problem(s)

10. If you are dealing with a customer in a prompt manner when addressing their complaints or issues, which of the following are you demonstrating?
    A. Assurance   B. Empathy
    C. Responsiveness   D. Reliability

11. Steve has recently been hired to work at the postal office in town. A customer comes into the office to complain about the number of packages of his they have lost over the past year.
When Steve attempts to help the upset customer, what should he make sure to do FIRST?
He should
    A. check into how legitimate the customer's complaints are and see if he can do anything about the missing packages
    B. just let the customer blow off some steam and chalk it up to an emotional outburst

C. ask for help from his boss to see how to handle the situation
D. assume the complaints are accurate and immediately attempt to correct them

12. How should a service representative react when a customer first presents them with a request?
    A. Apologize
    B. Greet them in a friendly manner
    C. Read from the employee handbook about the request
    D. Ask the customer to clarify information

13. In order to assuage a customer's frustration, which of the following should a civil service employee demonstrate?
    A. Compassion   B. Indifference   C. Surprise   D. Agreement

14. A customer comes into the office requesting that your organization do something for them that you know is not part of organization policy.
    Your FIRST responsibility would be to
    A. pass the customer on to higher management to deal with the issue
    B. persuade the customer to believe that the organization can grant their request
    C. mold expectations so they more closely resemble what the organization can do for the customer
    D. tell the customer there is no way you can comply with their request

15. Of the following potential distractors, which one MOST prevents a civil service employee from displaying good listening skills while a customer is speaking?
    A. Cell phones or checking e-mail
    B. Asking superfluous questions
    C. Background office noise
    D. Interrupting the customer to speak with colleagues

16. If you are in a situation where you have to deliver a negative response to a customer, it is often better to say _____ instead of just saying "no"?
    A. "I will try to…"   B. "You can…"
    C. "Our policy does not allow…" D. "I do not believe…"

17. You are working one-on-one with a customer.
    Which of the following would be the MOST appropriate body language to display?
    A. Make frowning faces
    B. Stare at a spot over the customer's shoulder
    C. Lean in toward the customer
    D. Cross your arms while they speak

18. The majority of communication in face-to-face meetings with customers is shown through
    A. word choice   B. tone
    C. clothing choice   D. body language

19. A customer angrily approaches you at your service desk and starts expressing his frustration with recent actions by your department.
Which of the following should be your FIRST responses to the customer?
   A. Listen to the person, then express understanding and apologize for how they have been negatively affected by your department's action
   B. Interrupt them while they are speaking and tell them to calm down or you will not help them
   C. Give them an explanation of why your department took the actions they did
   D. None of the above

19._____

20. Of the following services, which one is NOT customized to a specific individual's needs?
   A. Hair salon
   B. Elementary education
   C. Computer counseling
   D. Dental care

20._____

21. Which of the following civil service employees demonstrates excellent customer service?
   A. A park ranger who minimizes public interaction and contact
   B. The Postal Service employee who sees the customer as a commodity
   C. The office clerk who spends a lot of time with customers sharing personal stories and anecdotes
   D. A DMV employee with open body language and direct communication

21._____

22. It is important to have excellent knowledge of services and products, if applicable, when interacting with consumers because
   A. you can demonstrate your knowledge and impress the customer
   B. your organization can have a higher margin of profit regardless of customer benefit
   C. the customer's needs can best be matched with appropriate services/products
   D. you can look good to your superiors and keep your job

22._____

23. A park ranger has recently been coming to a kids' camp dirty and unkempt. Even though her job requires her to be outside at ties, why should she still care about her personal appearance?
   A. To speed up her service to the public
   B. So she is seen as a professional in her field
   C. It would help her organizational skills
   D. To show her level of expertise as a park ranger

23._____

24. How could guided conversation be a positive with interacting with the public?
   A. It allows you to anticipate a person's needs and expectations.
   B. Most people know what they want even before they show up to your office.
   C. It creates the impression of friendliness.
   D. It helps time move faster.

24._____

25. In the event a conflict or crisis arises, which of the following would be considered a POOR action to take when interacting with the public?   25._____
   A. Provide a constant flow of information
   B. Put the public's needs first
   C. Avoid saying "No Comment" as much as possible
   D. Assign multiple spokespeople so media calls can be dealt with efficiently

---

KEY (CORRECT ANSWERS)

1.	D	11.	A
2.	A	12.	D
3.	C	13.	A
4.	B	14.	C
5.	B	15.	D
6.	A	16.	B
7.	C	17.	C
8.	D	18.	D
9.	B	19.	A
10.	C	20.	B

21.	D
22.	C
23.	B
24.	A
25.	D

TEST 2

DIRECTIONS: Each question or incomplete statement is followed by several suggested answers or completions. Select the one that BEST answers the question or completes the statement. *PRINT THE LETTER OF THE CORRECT ANSWER IN THE SPACE AT THE RIGHT.*

1. John Smith answers a caller who struggles to understand a convoluted policy of your agency.
   How should he handle the customer's question?
   A. Tell the caller to go to the agency's website
   B. He should be honest and say he does not know the answer to the question
   C. John should explain the policy in general terms and refer them to a written version of the policy
   D. Tell the caller to talk to his supervisor and then give the caller the supervisor's extension

   1._____

2. While meeting with a group of young campers at the local parks and recreation office, you conduct a lecture on the importance of avoiding dangerous plants near the forest.
   What can you do to make sure your inexperienced audience remembers the main points of your presentation?
   A. Use flashy visuals that catch the eye
   B. Repeat and emphasize your points
   C. Make jokes so the presentation is livelier
   D. Allow the campers to ask questions at the end of the presentation

   2._____

3. A park ranger is about to deliver a speech at a public conservation meeting. Which of the following is the MOST important thing to keep in mind as he preps for the presentation?
   A. How large the audience is
   B. Whether or not he will be able to use visual aids
   C. If he will have time to use charts and graphs
   D. Audience interests

   3._____

4. Jerry receives a letter from a customer and is about to shred it without reading. When you stop him, he says that there is no reason to read it because you cannot learn very much from letters you receive from the public.
   Which of the following should you tell him in order to convince him that reading letters sent from the public is beneficial and necessary?
   A. These public letters can give us a feel for how we are meeting customer needs.
   B. Letters from the public tell us how well our informational efforts are working.
   C. These letters can inform us of what additional training we may need.
   D. The letters can tell us whether public information processes need to be changed or not.

   4._____

5. Ms. Johnson is a volunteer with the Parks and Recreation Department and her children also attend various summer programs through the district. She comes to you today to complain that one of her children was not allowed to join a program because they missed the sign-up by one day. She calls your staff a bunch of "morons" and complains that your department's actions are creating serious issues for her.
How should you handle this situation?
   A. Let Ms. Johnson rant until she gets it out of her system
   B. Tell her you cannot help her and will ask her to leave if she cannot stop referring to your colleagues as "morons"
   C. Refer Ms. Johnson to your boss
   D. Try to alter the tone of the conversation to a more objective and less emotional discussion of Ms. Johnson's problems

5._____

6. A civil service employee is tasked with moderating a town hall meeting regarding child safety, but he knows that residents will be attending the meeting with different motives.
How can the employee make sure the town hall meeting is as beneficial and informational as possible?
   A. Ask attendees to be open to changing their opinions and preferences
   B. Start out by recognizing the various motives but also stress the common objectives and interests
   C. Call out individuals who you know have specific reasons for attending and put them on the spot
   D. Cancel the meeting and avoid rescheduling it until you can be sure everyone is on the same page

6._____

7. During the question-and-answer session at the end of a presentation, a member of the public makes a suggestion that you deem not only practical but worthy of further discussion.
How should you react to this?
   A. Tell them you will let the appropriate people know of the suggestion
   B. Tell the person you concur with them wholeheartedly
   C. Let the person know you think it is a good idea but you cannot make decisions based on suggestions during Q and A
   D. Even though the suggestion is good, tell the person that someone in your organization has probably already thought of the idea

7._____

8. When in a conversation with a group of local residents, what is the BIGGEST problem with one or two people dominating the conversation?
   A. Your interaction could take longer than it should
   B. Some people will become distracted and not focus on the meeting anymore
   C. The other member of the group may not have an opportunity to share their opinions
   D. None of the above

8._____

9. You receive a phone call at the village hall, but the information being requested would need to come from the police station.
   How should you respond to the caller?
   A. Give them the police station's website and wish them well
   B. Tell them you are not responsible for their request
   C. Refer them to the police station's number and information
   D. Provide them with the information as best as you can

9._____

10. Which of the following should almost always be avoided when interacting with a member of the community?
    A. Contentious matters
    B. Topics about financial material
    C. Rules and regulations
    D. Technical lingo or jargon

10._____

11. When people use inflammatory language laced with obscenities, a town employee should
    A. refuse to continue the dialogue if the person cannot stop using the offensive language
    B. tell the person to talk to your supervisor
    C. allow the person to finish "venting" before attempting to find a solution to the problem
    D. hang up if on the phone; if in person, leave the area and ask the individual to leave as well

11._____

12. A member of the public has sent your agency a letter.
    Which of the following will help you figure out how much explaining you need to do when writing a response?
    A. Go to the agency website and search for how much explanation is provided there
    B. Take out the original customer letter and study it
    C. Presume the person who wrote the letter already has a working knowledge of the subject and thus will not require a lot of background explanation
    D. Look at past letters sent by your agency

12._____

13. During an informational meeting with local townspeople, a man makes a suggestion for a new town measure that is based on incorrect information and is impractical.
    What is the BEST way to handle a situation such as this?
    A. Ask if anyone else in attendance would like to respond to the suggestion
    B. Tell the person it is a great idea even though you are aware of its folly
    C. Thank the man for coming and tell everyone you always welcome their suggestions
    D. Inform the person that his/her comment clearly reflects an inferior knowledge about the subject

13._____

14. A member from the public calls your office about negative comments he has heard about one of your programs. You believe the comments were made by someone who had inaccurate material, but you are not completely certain of that because you are not directly involved with the program.

14._____

What is the BEST way to handle this situation?
- A. Tell the caller you will analyze the situation in depth and then call them back
- B. Tell the caller the evidence on which they have based their judgment is not supported
- C. Explain that your office has a "No Comment" policy regarding negative comments
- D. Let the caller know you are not involved with the program directly, and tell them to call the person who is

15. Which of the following quotes reflects the BEST way to handle an angry resident that keeps interrupting during a village meeting?
    - A. "I am here as a volunteer and I do not need this."
    - B. "I understand your anger, but we have quite a bit of information to cover tonight, so in fairness to everyone else, please let me continue."
    - C. "Every crowd has one black sheep in it."
    - D. "Sir, (or Ma'am) if you cannot stop interjecting, I will have security escort you from the premises."

16. Of the following, which is an example of nonverbal communication?
    - A. Frowning
    - B. Hand signs
    - C. A "21 Gun Salute"
    - D. All of the above

17. Residents of Masterton, Georgia, were recently made aware that the main road into and out of town will be under construction for the next four years. The construction will make travel time much more difficult for the citizens and they have demanded a meeting with your department. You are tasked with creating a presentation to explain to them why the construction is necessary.
    At the start of the presentation, you should
    - A. make a joke to lighten the mood
    - B. state the purpose of your presentation
    - C. provide a detailed account of the history behind the project
    - D. make a call to action

18. When a member of the public asks questions that are confusing or you do not understand right away, what is the BEST way to handle this situation?
    - A. Answer the question as you understand it
    - B. Stick to generalizations dealing with the subject of the question
    - C. Rephrase the question and ask the person if you understood what they were asking
    - D. Ask the person to repeat the question

19. When preparing for a public interaction, which of the following situations would be MOST appropriate to include handouts?
    - A. If you want to help the attendees remember important information after the interaction is over
    - B. If you want to keep the interaction short

C. When you want to remember key points to talk about
D. When you do not want attendees to have to pay attention during the interaction

20. John is in the process of handling a phone call when a local citizen approaches his desk to ask a question. Neither the caller nor the visitor seem to be in a crisis.
What should John do in this scenario?
    A. Keep talking with the caller until he is finished. Then tell the visitor he is sorry for making them wait.
    B. Remain on the phone with the caller but look up at the visitor every once and awhile so they know he has not forgotten about them.
    C. Tell the caller he has a visitor, so the conversation needs to end.
    D. Tell the visitor he will be with them as soon as he finishes the phone call.

21. When engaged in conversation with another person, which communication technique is MOST likely to ensure you comprehend fully what the other person to trying to communicate to you?
    A. Repeat back to the person what you think they are communicating
    B. Continual eye contact
    C. Making sure the person speaks slowly
    D. Nodding your head while they speak

22. You encounter someone who is frustrated about a situation and needs to vent by talking it out before they can move onto a productive conversation.
When a situation is like this, it is often BEST to
    A. recommend various strategies for calming down
    B. Ask to be excused from the conversation without offering why
    C. Explain to the person that it is unproductive to behave the way they are currently behaving
    D. Acknowledge that venting is a crucial step to moving past the emotions and allow the person to express his or her feelings

23. Which of the following is NOT an example of active listening?
    A. Taking notes
    B. Referring the customer to the manager after they are done speaking
    C. Using phrases like "I see" or "Go on"
    D. Repeating back to the customer what you've heard

24. Which of the following questions would be classified as a clarification question?
    A. "How long have you sold spoiled meat?"
    B. "Do you like our brand?"
    C. "You mentioned you liked this merchandise. How would you feel about this?"
    D. None of the above

25. When interacting with a member of the public, which of the following words should you avoid using as it is not positive as perceived by most people?
   A. "Absolutely"
   B. "You are welcome"
   C. "Here's what I can do"
   D. "I'll do my best"

KEY (CORRECT ANSWERS)

1.	C		11.	A
2.	B		12.	B
3.	D		13.	C
4.	A		14.	A
5.	D		15.	B
6.	B		16.	D
7.	A		17.	B
8.	C		18.	C
9.	C		19.	A
10.	D		20.	D

21.	A
22.	D
23.	B
24.	C
25.	D

EXAMINATION SECTION
TEST 1

DIRECTIONS: Each question or incomplete statement is followed by several suggested answers or completions. Select the one that BEST answers the question or completes the statement. *PRINT THE LETTER OF THE CORRECT ANSWER IN THE SPACE AT THE RIGHT.*

1. Good procedure in handling complaints from the public may be divided into the following four principal stages:
   I. Investigation of the complaint
   II. Receipt of the complaint
   III. Assignment of responsibility for investigation and correction
   IV. Notification of correction

   The ORDER in which these stages ordinarily come is:
   A. III, II, I, IV   B. II, III, I, IV   C. II, III, IV, I   D. II, IV, III, I

   1.____

2. The department may expect the MOST severe public criticism if
   A. it asks for an increase in its annual budget
   B. it purchases new and costly street cleaning equipment
   C. sanitation officers and men are reclassified to higher salary grades
   D. there is delay in cleaning streets of snow

   2.____

3. The MOST important function of public relations in the department should be to
   A. develop cooperation on the part of the public in keeping streets clean
   B. get stricter penalties enacted for health code violations
   C. recruit candidates for entrance positions who ca be developed into supervisors
   D. train career personnel so that they can advance in the department

   3.____

4. The one of the following which has MOST frequently elicited unfavorable public comment has been
   A. dirty sidewalks or streets   B. dumping on lot
   C. failure to curb dogs   D. overflowing garbage cans

   4.____

5. It has been suggested that, as a public relations measure, sections hold *open house* for the public.
   The MOST effective time for this would be
   A. during the summer when children are not in school and can accompany their parents
   B. during the winter when show is likely to fall and the public can see snow removal preparations
   C. immediately after a heavy snow storm when department snow removal operations are in full progress
   D. when street sanitation is receiving general attention as during *Keep City Clean* week

   5.____

43

6. When a public agency conducts a public relations program, it is MOST likely to find that each recipient of its message will
   A. disagree with the basic purpose of the message if the officials are not well known to him
   B. accept the message if it is presented by someone perceived as having a definite intention to persuade
   C. ignore the message unless it is presented in a literate and clever manner
   D. give greater attention to certain portions of the message as a result of his individual and cultural differences

7. Following are three statements about public relations and communications:
   I. A person who seeks to influence public opinion can speed up a trend
   II. Mass communications is the exposure of a mass audience to an idea
   III. All media are equally effective in reaching opinion leaders
   Which of the following choices CORRECTLY classifies the above statements into those which are correct and those which are not?
   A. I and II are correct, but III is not.
   B. II and III are correct, but I is not.
   C. I and III are correct, but II is not.
   D. III is correct, but I and II are not.

8. Public relations experts say that MAXIMUM effect for a message results from
   A. concentrating in one medium
   B. ignoring mass media and concentrating on *opinion makers*
   C. presenting only those factors which support a given position
   D. using a combination of two or more of the available media

9. To assure credibility and avoid hostility, the public relations man MUST
   A. make certain his message is truthful, not evasive or exaggerated
   B. make sure his message contains some dire consequence if ignored
   C. repeat the message often enough so that it cannot be ignored
   D. try to reach as many people and groups as possible

10. The public relations man MUST be prepared to assume that members of his audience
    A. may have developed attitudes toward his proposals—favorable, neutral, or unfavorable
    B. will be immediately hostile
    C. will consider his proposals with an open mind
    D. will invariably need an introduction to his subject

11. The one of the following statements that is CORRECT is:
    A. When a stupid question is asked of you by the public, it should be disregarded
    B. If you insist on formality between you and the public, the public will not be able to ask stupid questions that cannot be answered
    C. The public should be treated courteously, regardless of how stupid their questions may be
    D. You should explain to the public how stupid their questions are

12. With regard to public relations, the MOST important item which should be emphasized in an employee training program is that
    A. each inspector is a public relations agent
    B. an inspector should give the public all the information it asks for
    C. it is better to make mistakes and give erroneous information than to tell the public that you do not know the correct answer to their problem
    D. public relations is so specialized a field that only persons specially trained in it should consider it

12.____

13. Members of the public frequently ask about departmental procedures.
    Of the following, it is BEST to
    A. advise the public to put the question in writing so that he can get a proper formal reply
    B. refuse to answer because this is a confidential matter
    C. explain the procedure as briefly as possible
    D. attempt to avoid the issue by discussing other matters

13.____

14. The effectiveness of a public relations program in a public agency such as the authority is BEST indicated by the
    A. amount of mass media publicity favorable to the policies of the authority
    B. morale of those employees who directly serve the patrons of the authority
    C. public's understanding and support of the authority's program and policies
    D. number of complaint received by the authority from patrons using its facilities

14.____

15. In an attempt to improve public opinion about a certain idea, the BEST course of action for an agency to take would be to present the
    A. clearest statements of the idea even though the language is somewhat technical
    B. idea as the result of long-term studies
    C. idea in association with something familiar to most people
    D. idea as the viewpoint of the majority leaders

15.____

16. The fundamental factor in any agency's community relations program is
    A. an outline of the objectives
    B. relations with the media
    C. the everyday actions of the employees
    D. a well-planned supervisory program

16.____

17. The FUNDAMENTAL factor in the success of a community relations program is
    A. true commitment by the community
    B. true commitment by the administration
    C. a well-planned, systematic approach
    D. the actions of individuals in their contacts with the public

17.____

18. The statement below which is LEAST correct is:
    A. Because of selection standards, the supervisor frequently encounters problems resulting from subordinates' inability to express themselves in the language of the profession.
    B. Distortion of the meaning of a communication is usually brought about by a failure to use language that has a precise meaning to others.
    C. The term *filtering* is the distortion or dilution of content of a communication that occurs as information is passed from individual to individual.
    D. The complexity of the *communications net* will directly affect.

19. Consider the following three statements that may or may not be CORRECT:
    I. In order to prevent the stifling of communications flow, supervisors should insist that employees use the formal communications network.
    II. Two-way communications are faster and more accurate than one-way communications.
    III. There is a direct correlation between the effectiveness of communications and the total setting in which they occur.
    The choice below which MOST accurately describes the above statement is:
    A. All three are correct.
    B. All three are incorrect.
    C. More than one statement is correct.
    D. Only one of the statements is correct.

20. The statement below which is MOST inaccurate is:
    A. The supervisor's most important tool in learning whether or not he is communicating well is feedback.
    B. Follow-up is essential if useful feedback is to be obtained.
    C. Subordinates are entitled, as a matter of right, to explanations from management concerning the reasons for orders or directives.
    D. A skilled supervisor is often able to use the grapevine to good advantage.

21. *Since concurrence by those affected is not sought, this kind of communication can be issued with relative ease.*
    The kind of communication being referred to in this quotation is
    A. autocratic B. democratic C. directive D. free-rein

22. The statement below which is LEAST correct is:
    A. Clarity is more important in oral communicating than in written since the readers of a written communication can read it over again.
    B. Excessive use of abbreviations in written communications should be avoided.
    C. Short sentences with simple words are preferred over complex sentences and difficult words in a written communication.
    D. The *newspaper* style of writing ordinarily simplifies expression and facilitates understanding.

23. Which one of the following is the MOST important factor for the department to consider in building a good public image?
    A. A good working relationship with the news media
    B. An efficient community relations program
    C. An efficient system for handling citizen complaints
    D. The proper maintenance of facilities and equipment
    E. The behavior of individuals in their contacts with the public.

24. It has been said that the ability to communicate clearly and concisely is the MOST important single skill of the supervisor.
    Consider the following statements:
    I. The adage, *Actions speak louder than words*, has NO application in superior/subordinate communications since good communications are accomplished with words.
    II. The environment in which a communication takes place will *rarely* determine its effect.
    III. Words are symbolic representations which must be associated with past experience or else they are meaningless.
    The choice below which MOST accurately describes the above statements is:
    A. I, II, and III are correct.
    B. I and II are correct, but III is not.
    C. I and III are correct, but II is not.
    D. III is correct, but I and II are not.
    E. I, II, and III are incorrect.

25. According to expert opinion, the effectiveness of an organization is very dependent upon good upward, downward, and lateral communications. Lateral communications are most important to the activity of coordinating the efforts of organizational units. Before real communication can take place at any level, barriers to communication must be recognized, understood, and removed.
    Consider the following three statements:
    I. The *principal* barrier to good communications is a failure to establish empathy between sender and receiver.
    II. The difference in status or rank between the sender and receiver of a communication may be a communications barrier.
    III. Communications are easier if they travel upward from subordinate to superior
    The choice below which MOST accurately describes the above statements is:
    A. I, II and III are incorrect.
    B. I and II are incorrect.
    C. I, II, and III are correct.
    D. I and II are correct.
    E. I and III are incorrect.

KEY (CORRECT ANSWERS)

1.	B	11.	C
2.	D	12.	A
3.	A	13.	C
4.	A	14.	C
5.	D	15.	C
6.	D	16.	C
7.	A	17.	D
8.	D	18.	A
9.	A	19.	D
10.	A	20.	C

21.	A
22.	A
23.	E
24.	D
25.	E

CODING

EXAMINATION SECTION

TEST 1

COMMENTARY

An ingenious question-type called coding, involving elements of alphabetizing, filing, name and number comparison, and evaluative judgment and application, has currently won wide acceptance in testing circles for measuring clerical aptitude and general ability, particularly on the senior (middle) grades (levels).

While the directions for this question-type usually vary in detail, the candidate is generally asked to consider groups of names, codes, and numbers, and, then, according to a given plan, to arrange codes in alphabetic order; to arrange these in numerical sequence; to rearrange columns of names and numbers in correct order; to espy errors in coding; to choose the correct coding arrangement in consonance with the given directions and examples, etc.

This question-type appears to have few parameters in respect to form, substance, or degree of difficulty.

Accordingly, acquaintance with, and practice in the coding question is recommended for the serious candidate.

DIRECTIONS: Column I consists of serial numbers of dollar bills. Column II shows different ways of arranging the corresponding serial numbers.
The serial numbers of dollar bills in Column I begin and end with a capital letter and have an eight-digit number in between. The serial numbers in Column I are to be arranged according to the following rules:
First: In alphabetical order according to the first letter.
Second: When two or more serial numbers have the same first letter, in alphabetical order according to the last letter.
Third: When two or more serial numbers have the same first and last letters, in numerical order, beginning with the lowest number.

The serial numbers in Column I are numbered (1) through (5) in the order in which they are listed. In Column II, the numbers (1) through (5) are arranged in four different ways to show different arrangements of the corresponding serial numbers. Choose the answer in Column II in which the serial numbers are arranged according to the above rules.

Column I

1. E75044127B
2. B96399104A
3. B93939086A
4. B47064465H

Column II

A. 4, 1, 3, 2, 5
B. 4, 1, 2, 3, 5
C. 4, 3, 2, 5, 1
D. 3, 2, 5, 4, 1

In the simple question, the four serial numbers starting with B should be put before the serial number starting with E. The serial numbers starting with B and ending with A should be put before the serial number starting with B and ending with H. The three serial numbers starting with B and ending with A should be listed in numerical order, beginning with the lowest

49

2 (#1)

number. The correct way to arrange the serial numbers, therefore, is:
3. B93939086A
2. B96399104A
5. B99040922A
4. B47064465H
1. E75044127B

Since the order of arrangement is 3, 2, 5, 4, 1, the answer to the sample question is D.

Column I   Column II

1. 1. D89143888P   A. 3, 5, 2, 1, 4   1.____
    2. D98143838B   B. 3, 1, 4, 5, 2
    3. D89113883B   C. 4, 2, 3, 1, 5
    4. D89148338P   D. 4, 1, 3, 5, 2
    5. D89148388B

2. 1. W62455590E   A. 2, 4, 3, 1, 5   2.____
    2. W62455090F   B. 3, 1, 5, 2, 4
    3. W62405099E   C. 5, 3, 1, 4, 2
    4. V62455097F   D. 5, 4, 3, 1, 2
    5. V62405979E

3. 1. N74663826M   A. 2, 4, 5, 3, 1   3.____
    2. M74633286M   B. 2, 5, 4, 1, 3
    3. N76633228N   C. 1, 2, 5, 3, 4
    4. M76483686N   D. 2, 5, 1, 4, 3
    5. M74636688M

4. 1. P97560324B   A. 1, 5, 2, 3, 4   4.____
    2. R97663024B   B. 3, 1, 4, 5, 2
    3. P97503024E   C. 1, 5, 3, 2, 4
    4. R97563240E   D. 1, 5, 2, 3, 4
    5. P97652304B

5. 1. H92411165G   A. 2, 5, 3, 4, 1   5.____
    2. A92141465G   B. 3, 4, 2, 5, 1
    3. H92141165C   C. 3, 2, 1, 5, 4
    4. H92444165C   D. 3, 1, 2, 5, 4
    5. A92411465G

6. 1. X90637799S   A. 4, 3, 5, 2, 1   6.____
    2. N90037696S   B. 5, 4, 2, 1, 3
    3. Y90677369B   C. 5, 2, 4, 1, 3
    4. X09677693B   D. 5, 2, 3, 4, 1
    5. M09673699S

3 (#1)

Column I   Column II

7. 1. K78425174L   A. 4, 2, 1, 3, 5   7._____
    2. K78452714C   B. 2, 3, 5, 4, 1
    3. K78547214N   C. 1, 4, 2, 3, 5
    4. K78442774C   D. 4, 2, 1, 5, 3
    5. K78547724M

8. 1. P18736652U   A. 1, 3, 4, 5, 2   8._____
    2. P18766352V   B. 1, 5, 2, 3, 4
    3. T17686532U   C. 3, 4, 5, 1, 2
    4. T17865523U   D. 5, 2, 1, 3, 4
    5. P18675332V

9. 1. L51138101K   A. 1, 5, 3, 2, 4   9._____
    2. S51138001R   B. 1, 3, 5, 2, 4
    3. S51188222K   C. 1, 5, 1, 4, 3
    4. S51183110R   D. 2, 5, 1, 4, 3
    5. L51188100R

10. 1. J28475336   A. 5, 1, 2, 3, 4   10._____
    2. T28775363D   B. 4, 3, 5, 1, 2
    3. J27843566P   C. 1, 5, 2, 4, 3
    4. T27834563P   D. 5, 1, 3, 2, 4
    5. J2843553D

11. 1. S55126179E   A. 1, 5, 2, 3, 4   11._____
    2. R51336177Q   B. 3, 4, 1, 5, 2
    3. P55126177R   C. 3, 5, 2, 1, 4
    4. S55126178R   D. 4, 3, 1, 5, 2
    5. R55126180P

12. 1. T64217813Q   A. 4, 1, 3, 2, 4   12._____
    2. I64217817O   B. 2, 4, 3, 1, 5
    3. T64217818O   C. 4, 1, 5, 2, 3
    4. I64217811Q   D. 2, 3, 4, 1, 5
    5. T64217816Q

13. 1. B33886897B   A. 5, 1, 3, 4, 2   13._____
    2. B38386882B   B. 1, 2, 5, 3, 4
    3. D33389862B   C. 1, 2, 5, 4, 3
    4. D33336887D   D. 2, 1, 4, 5, 3
    5. B38888697D

14. 1. E11664554M   A. 4, 1, 2, 5, 3   14._____
    2. F11164544M   B. 2, 4, 1, 5, 3
    3. F11614455N   C. 4, 2, 1, 3, 5
    4. E11665454M   D. 1, 4, 2, 3, 5
    5. F16161545N

51

4 (#1)

	Column I	Column II	
15.	1. C86611355W 2. C68631533V 3. G88631533V 4. C68833515V 5. G68833511W	A. 2, 4, 1, 5, 3 B. 1, 2, 4, 3, 5 C. 1, 2, 5, 4, 3 D. 1, 2, 4, 3, 5	15.____
16.	1. R73665312J 2. P73685512J 3. P73968511J 4. R73665321K 5. R63985211K	A. 3, 2, 1, 4, 5 B. 2, 3, 5, 1, 4 C. 2, 3, 1, 5, 4 D. 3, 1, 5, 2, 4	16.____
17.	1. X33661222U 2. Y83961323V 3. Y88991123V 4. X33691233U 5. X38691333U	A. 1, 4, 5, 2, 3 B. 4, 5, 1, 3, 2 C. 4, 5, 1, 2, 3 D. 4, 1, 5, 2, 3	17..____
18.	1. B22838847W 2. B28833874V 3. B22288344X 4. B28238374V 5. B28883347V	A. 4, 5, 2, 3, 1 B. 4, 2, 5, 1, 3 C. 4, 5, 2, 1, 3 D. 4, 1, 5, 2, 3	18.____
19.	1. H44477447G 2. H47444777G 3. H74777477C 4. H44747447G 5. H77747447C	A. 1, 3, 5, 4, 2 B. 3, 1, 5, 2, 4 C. 1, 4, 2, 3, 5 D. 3, 5, 1, 4, 2	19.____
20.	1. G11143447G 2. G15133388C 3. C15134378G 4. G11534477C 5. C15533337C	A. 3, 5, 1, 4, 2 B. 1, 4, 3, 2, 5 C. 5, 3, 4, 2, 1 D. 4, 3, 1, 2, 5	20.____
21.	1. J96693369F 2. J66939339F 3. J96693693E 4. J966T3933E 5. J69639363F	A. 4, 3, 2, 5, 1 B. 2, 5, 4, 1, 3 C. 2, 5, 4, 3, 1 D. 3, 4, 5, 2, 1	21.____
22.	1. L15567834Z 2. P11587638Z 3. M51567688Z 4. O55578784Z 5. N53588783Z	A. 3, 1, 5, 2, 4 B. 1, 3, 5, 4, 2 C. 1, 3, 5, 2, 4 D. 3, 1, 4, 4, 2	22.____

	Column I	Column II

	Column I		Column II	
23.	1. C83261824G 2. C78361822C 3. G83261732G 4. C88261823C 5. G83261743C	A. B. C. D.	2, 4, 1, 5, 3 4, 2, 1, 3, 5 3, 1, 5, 2, 4 , 3, 5, 1, 4	23.____
24.	1. A11710107H 2. H17110017A 3. A11170707A 4. H17170171H 5. A11710177A	A. B. C. D.	2, 1, 4, 3, 5 3, 1, 5, 2, 4 3, 4, 1, 5, 2 3, 5, 1, 2, 4	24.____
25.	1. R26794821S 2. O26794821T 3. M26794821Z 4. Q26794821R 5. S26794821P	A. B. C. D.	3, 2, 4, 1, 5 3, 4, 2, 1, 5 4, 2, 1, 3, 5 5, 4, 1, 2, 3	25.____

KEY (CORRECT ANSWERS)

1.	A	11.	C
2.	D	12.	B
3.	B	13.	B
4.	C	14.	D
5.	A	15.	A
6.	C	16.	C
7.	D	17.	A
8.	B	18.	B
9.	A	19.	D
10.	D	20.	C

21.	A
22.	B
23.	A
24.	D
25.	A

TEST 2

Questions 1-5.

DIRECTIONS: Questions 1 through 5 consist of a set of letters and numbers located under Column I. For each question, pick the answer (A, B, C, or D) located under Column II which contains ONLY letters and numbers that appear in the question in Column II. *PRINT THE LETTER OF THE CORRECT ANSWER IN THE SPACE AT THE RIGHT.*

SAMPLE QUESTION

Column I

B-9-P-H-2-Z-N-8-4-M

Column II

A. B-4-C-3-R-9
B. 4-H-P-8-6-N
C. P-2-Z-8-M-9
D. 4-B-N-5-E-Z

Choice C is the correct answer because P,2,Z,8,M and 9 all appear in the sample question. All the other choices have at least one letter or number that is not in the question.

Column I

1. 1-7-6-J-L-T-3-S-A-2

2. C-0-Q-5-3-9-H-L-2-7

3. P-3-B-C-5-6-0-E-1-T

4. U-T-Z-2-4-S-8-6-B-3

5. 4-D-F-G-C-6-8-3-J-L

Column II

1. A. J-3-S-A-7-L
   B. T-S-A-2-6-5
   C. 3-7-J-L-S-Z
   D. A-7-4-J-L-1

2. A. F-9-T-2-7-Q
   B. 3-0-6-9-L-C
   C. 9-L-7-Q-C-3
   D. H-Q-4-5-9-7

3. A. B-4-6-1-3-T
   B. T-B-P-3-E-0
   C. 5-3-0-E-B-G
   D. 0-6-P-T-9-B

4. A. 2-4-S-V-Z-3
   B. B-Z-S-8-3-6
   C. 4-T-U-8-L-B
   D. 9-3-T-Z-1-2

5. A. T-D-6-8-4-J
   B. C-4-3-2-J-F
   C. 8-3-C-5-G-6
   D. C-8-6-J-G-L

1._____

2._____

3._____

4._____

5._____

Questions 6-12.

DIRECTIONS: Each of the questions numbered 6 through 12 consist of a long series of letters and numbers under Column I and four short series of letters and numbers under Column II. For each question, choose the short series of letters and numbers which is entirely and exactly the same as some part of the long series.

Column I   Column II

6. IE227FE383L4700   A. E27FE3   6._____
                              B. EF838L
                              C. EL4700
                              D. 83LE70

7. 77J646G54NPB318   A. NPB318   7._____
                              B. J646J5
                              C. 4G54NP
                              D. C54NPB

8. 85887T358W24A93   A. 858887   8._____
                              B. W24A93
                              C. 858W24
                              D. 87T353

9. E104RY796B33H14   A. 04RY79   9._____
                              B. E14RYR
                              C. 96B3H1
                              D. RY7996

10. W58NP12141DE07M   A. 8MP121   10._____
                              B. W58NP1
                              C. 14DEO7
                              D. 12141D

11. P473R365M442V5W   A. P47365   11._____
                              B. 73P365
                              C. 365M44
                              D. 5X42V5

12. 865CG441V21SS59   A. 1V12SS   12._____
                              B. V21SS5
                              C. 5GC441
                              D. 894CG4

KEY (CORRECT ANSWERS)

1. A
2. C
3. B
4. B
5. D
6. D
7. A
8. B
9. A
10. D
11. C
12. B

TEST 3

DIRECTIONS: Each question from 1 through 8 consists of a set of letters and numbers. For each question, pick as your answer from the column to the right the choice has ONLY numbers and letters that are in the question you are answering.

To help you understand what to do, the following sample question is given:

SAMPLE: B-9-P-H-2-Z-N-8-4-M

A. B-4-C-3-E-9
B. 4-H-P-8-6-N
C. P-2-Z-8-M-9
D. 4-B-N-R-E-A

Choice C is the correct answer because P, 2, Z, 8, M-9 are in the sample question. All the other choices have at least one letter or number that is not in the question.

Questions 1 through 4 are based on Column I.

Column I

1. X-8-3-I-H-9-4-G-P-U   A. I-G-W-8-2-1   1.____
2. 4-1-2-X-U-B-9-H-7-3   B. U-3-G-9-P-8   2.____
3. U-I-G-2-5-4-W-P-3-B   C. 3-G-I-4-S-U   3.____
4. 3-H-7-G-4-5-1-U-B   D. 9-X-4-7-2-H   4.____

Questions 5 through 8 are based on Column II.

Column II

5. L-2-9-Z-R-8-Q-Y-5-7   A. 8-R-N-3-T-Z   5.____
6. J-L-9-N-Y-8-5-Q-Z-2   B. 2-L-R-5-7-Q   6.____
7. T-Y-3-3-J-Q-2-N-R-Z   C. J-2-8-Z-T-5   7.____
8. 8-Z-7-T-N-L-1-E-R-3   D. Z-8-9-3-L-5   8.____

KEY (CORRECT ANSWERS)

1. B 5. B
2. D 6. C
3. C 7. A
4. C 8. A

TEST 4

DIRECTIONS: Questions 1 through 5 have lines of letters and numbers. Each letter should be matched with its number in accordance with the following table.

Letter:	F	R	C	A	W	L	E	N	B	T
Matching Number:	0	1	2	3	4	5	6	7	8	9

From the table you can determine that the letter F has the matching number 0 below it, the letter R has the matching number 1 below it, etc.

For each question, compare each line of letters and numbers carefully to see if each letter has its correct matching number. If all the letters and numbers are matched correctly in none of the line of the question, mark your answer A; only one of the lines in the question, mark your answer B; only two of the lines of the question, mark your answer C; all three lines of the question, mark your answer D.

    WBCR   4826
    TLBF   9580
    ATNE   3986

There is a mistake in the first line because the letter R should have its matching number 1 instead of the number 6. The second line is correct because each letter shown has the correct matching number.
There is a mistake in the third line because the letter N should have the matching number 7 instead of the number 8. Since all the letters and numbers are matched correctly in only one of the lines in the sample, the correct answer is B.

1. EBCT   6829   1.____
    ATWR   3962
    NLBW   7584

2. RNCT   1729   2.____
    LNCR   5728
    WAEB   5368

3. STWB   7948   3.____
    RABL   1385
    TAEF   9360

4. LWRB   5417   4.____
    RLWN   1647
    CBWA   2843

5. ABTC   3792   5.____
    WCER   5261
    AWCN   3417

KEY (CORRECT ANSWERS)

1. C
2. B
3. D
4. B
5. A

TEST 5

DIRECTIONS: Assume that each of the capital letters in the table below represents the name of an employee enrolled in the city employees' retirement system. The number directly beneath the letter represents the agency for which the employee works, and the small letter directly beneath represents the code for the employee's account.

Name of Employee:	L	O	T	Q	A	M	R	N	C
Agency:	3	4	5	9	8	7	52	1	6
Account Code:	r	f	b	i	d	t	g	e	n

In each of the following Questions 1 through 10, the agency code numbers and the account code letters in Columns 2 and 3 should correspond to the capital letters in Column 1 and should be in the same consecutive order. For each question, look at each column carefully and mark your answer as follows:
    if there are one or more errors in Column 2 only, mark your answer A;
    if there are one or more errors in Column 3 only, mark your answer B;
    if there are one or more error in Column 2 and one or more errors in Column 3, mark your answer C;
    if there are NO errors in either column, mark your answer D.

The following sample question is given to help you understand the procedure.

Column 1	Column 2	Column 3
TQLMOC	583746	birtfn

In Column 2, the second agency code number (corresponding to letter Q) should be "9," not "8." Column 3 is coded correctly to Column 1. Since there is an error only in Column 2, the correct answer is A.

	Column 1	Column 2	Column 3	
1.	QLNRCA	931268	ifegnd	1._____
2.	NRMOTC	127546	egftbn	2._____
3.	RCTALM	265837	gndbrt	3._____
4.	TAMLON	578341	bdtrfe	4._____
5.	ANTROM	815427	debigt	5._____
6.	MRALON	728341	tgdrfe	6._____
7.	CTNQRO	657924	ndeigf	7._____
8.	QMROTA	972458	itgfbd	8._____

	Column 1	Column 2	Column 3	
9.	RQMCOL	297463	gitnfr	9.___
10.	NOMRTQ	147259	eftgbi	10.___

KEY (CORRECT ANSWERS)

1. D   6. D
2. C   7. C
3. B   8. D
4. A   9. A
5. B   10. D

TEST 6

DIRECTIONS: Each of Questions 1 through 6 consist of three lines of code letters and numbers. The numbers on each line should correspond to the code letter on the same line in accordance with the table below.

Code Letter:	D	Y	K	L	P	U	S	R	A	E
Corresponding Number:	0	1	2	3	4	5	6	7	8	9

On some of the lines an error exists in the coding. Prepare the letters and numbers in each question carefully. If you find an error or errors on
  only one of the lines in the question, mark your answer A;
  any two lines in the question, mark your answer B;
  all three lines in the question, mark your answer C;
  none of the lines in the question, mark your answer D.

SAMPLE QUESTION
  KSRYELD   2671930
  SAPUEKL   6845913
  RYKADLP   5128034

In the above sample, the first line is correct since each code letter listed has the correct corresponding number. On the second line, an error exists because code letter R should have the number 2 instead of number 1. On the third line, an error exists because the code letter R should have the number 7 instead of the number 5. Since there are errors on two of the three lines, the correct answer is B.

Now answer the following questions using the same procedure.

1. YPUSRLD   1456730
    UPSAEDY   5648901
    PREYDKS   4791026

2. AERLPUS   8973456
    DKLYDPA   0231048
    UKLDREP   5230794

3. DAPUSLA   0845683
    YKLDLPS   1230356
    PUSKYDE   4562101

4. LRPUPDL   3745403
    SUPLEDR   6543907
    PKEYDLU   4291025

5. KEYDESR   2910967
    PRSALEY   4678391
    LRAYSK   3687162

6. YESREYL   1967913
   PLPRAKY   4346821
   YLPSRDU   1346705

6.____

KEY (CORRECT ANSWERS)

1. A   4. A
2. D   5. B
3. C   6. A

CODING

COMMENTARY

An ingenious question-type called coding, involving elements of alphabetizing, filing, name and number comparison, and evaluative judgment and application, has currently won wide acceptance in testing circles for measuring clerical aptitude and general ability, particularly on the senior (middle) grades (levels).

While the directions for this question usually vary in detail, the candidate is generally asked to consider groups of names, codes, and numbers, and, then, according to a given plan, to arrange codes in alphabetic order; to arrange these in numerical sequence; to re-arrange columns of names and numbers in correct order; to espy errors in coding; to choose the correct coding arrangement in consonance with the given directions and examples, etc.

This question-type appears to have few paramaters in respect to form, substance, or degree of difficulty.

Accordingly, acquaintance with, and practice in, the coding question is recommended for the serious candidate.

EXAMINATION SECTION
TEST 1

DIRECTIONS:

```
                           CODE TABLE
Name of Applicant       H A N G S B R U K E
Test Code               c o m p l e x i t y
File Number             0 1 2 3 4 5 6 7 8 9
```

Assume that each of the above *capital letters* is the first letter of the Name of an Applicant, that the *small letter* directly beneath each capital letter is the Test Code for the Applicant, and that the *number* directly beneath each code letter is the File Number for the Applicant.

In each of the following questions, the test code letters and the file numbers in Columns 2 and 3 should correspond to the capital letters in Column 1. For each question, look at each column carefully and mark your answer as follows:

If there is an error only in Column 2, mark your answer A.
If there is an error only in Column 3, mark your answer B.
If there is an error in both Columns 2 and 3, mark your answer C.
If both Columns 2 and 3 are correct, mark your answer D.

The following sample question is given to help you understand the procedure.

SAMPLE QUESTION

Column 1	Column 2	Column 3
AKEHN	otyci	18902

In Column 2, the final test code letter "i" should be "m." Column 3 is correctly coded to Column 1. Since there is an error only in Column 2, the answer is A

	Column 1	Column 2	Column 3	
1.	NEKKU	mytti	29987	1._____
2.	KRAEB	txlye	86095	2._____
3.	ENAUK	ymoit	92178	3._____
4.	REANA	xeomo	69121	4._____
5.	EKHSE	ytcxy	97049	5._____

KEY (CORRECT ANSWERS)

1. B
2. C
3. D
4. A
5. C

TEST 2

DIRECTIONS: The employee identification codes in Column I begin and end with a capital letter and have an eight-digit number in between. In Questions 1 through 8, employee identification codes in Column I are to be arranged according to the following rules:

First: Arrange in alphabetical order according to the first letter.

Second: When two or more employee identification codes have the same first letter, arrange in alphabetical order according to the last letter.

Third: When two or more employee codes have the same first and last letters, arrange in numerical order beginning with the lowest number.

The employee identification codes in Column I are numbered 1 through 5 in the order in which they are listed. In Column II the numbers 1 through 5 are arranged in four different ways to show different arrangements of the corresponding employee identification numbers. Choose the answer in Column II in which the employee identification numbers are arranged according to the above rules.

SAMPLE QUESTION

Column I	Column II
1. E75044127B	A. 4, 1, 3, 2, 5
2. B96399104A	B. 4, 1, 2, 3, 5
3. B93939086A	C. 4, 3, 2, 5, 1
4. B47064465H	D. 3, 2, 5, 4, 1
5. B99040922A	

In the sample question, the four employee identification codes starting with B should be put before the employee identification code starting with E. The employee identification codes starting with B and ending with A should be put before the employee identification codes starting with B and ending with H. The three employee identification codes starting with B and ending with A should be listed in numerical order, beginning with the lowest number. The correct way to arrange the employee identification codes, therefore, is 3, 2, 5, 4, 1 shown below.

3. B93939086A
2. B96399104A
5. B99040922A
4. B47064465H
1. E75044127B

Therefore, the answer to the sample question is D. Now answer the following questions according to the above rules.

Column I	Column II
1. 1. G42786441J	A. 2, 5, 4, 3, 1
2. H45665413J	B. 5, 4, 1, 3, 2
3. G43117690J	C. 4, 5, 1, 3, 2
4. G43546698I	D. 1, 3, 5, 4, 2
5. G41679942I	

1.____

2 (#2)

2. 1. S44556178T   A. 1, 3, 5, 2, 4   2.____
    2. T43457169T   B. 4, 3, 5, 2, 1
    3. S53321176T   C. 5, 3, 1, 2, 4
    4. T53317998S   D. 5, 1, 3, 4, 2
    5. S67673942S

3. 1. R63394217D   A. 5, 4, 2, 3, 1   3.____
    2. R63931247D   B. 1, 5, 3, 2, 4
    3. R53931247D   C. 5, 3, 1, 2, 4
    4. R66874239D   D. 5, 1, 2, 3, 4
    4. R46799366D

4. 1. A35671968B   A. 3, 2, 1, 4, 5   4.____
    2. A35421794C   B. 2, 3, 1, 5, 4
    3. A35466987B   C. 1, 3, 2, 4, 5
    4. C10435779A   D. 3, 1, 2, 4, 5
    5. C00634779B

5. 1. I99746426Q   A. 2, 1, 3, 5, 4   5.____
    2. I10445311Q   B. 5, 4, 2, 1, 3
    3. J63749877P   C. 4, 5, 3, 2, 1
    4. J03421739Q   D. 2, 1, 4, 5, 3
    5. J00765311Q

6. 1. M33964217N   A. 4, 1, 5, 2, 3   6.____
    2. N33942770N   B. 5, 1, 4, 3, 2
    3. N06155881M   C. 4, 1, 5, 3, 2
    4. M00433669M   D. 1, 4, 5, 2, 3
    5. M79034577N

7. 1. D77643905C   A. 1, 2, 5, 3, 4   7.____
    2. D44106788C   B. 5, 3, 2, 1, 4
    3. D13976022F   C. 2, 1, 5, 3, 4
    4. D97655430E   D. 2, 1, 4, 5, 3
    5. D00439776F

8. 1. W22746920A   A. 2, 1, 3, 4, 5   8.____
    2. W22743720A   B. 2, 1, 5, 3, 4
    3. W32987655A   C. 1, 2, 3, 4, 5
    4. W43298765A   D. 1, 2, 5, 3, 4
    5. W30987433A

KEY (CORRECT ANSWERS)

1. B   5. A
2. D   6. C
3. C   7. D
4. D   8. B

TEST 3

DIRECTIONS: Each of the following equestions consists of three sets of names and name codes. In each question, the two names and name codes on the same line are supposed to be exactly the same.

Look carefully at each set of names and codes and mark your answer:
- A. if there are mistakes in all three sets
- B. if there are mistakes in two of the sets
- C. if there is a mistake in only one set
- D. if there are no mistakes in any of the sets

The following sample question is given to help you understand the procedure.

Macabe, John N. - V	53162	Macade, John N. - V	53162
Howard, Joan S. - J	24791	Howard, Joan S. - J	24791
Ware, Susan B. - A	45068	Ware, Susan B. - A	45968

In the above sample question, the names and name codes of the first set are not exactly the same because of the spelling of the last name (Macabe - Macade). The names and name codes of the second set are exactly the same. The names and name codes of the third set are not exactly the same because the two name codes are different (A 45068 - A 45968), Since there are mistakes in only 2 of the sets, the answer to the sample question is B.

1. Powell, Michael C. - 78537 F   Powell, Michael C. - 78537 F
   Martinez, Pablo, J. - 24435 P   Martinez, Pablo J. - 24435 P
   MacBane, Eliot M. - 98674 E   MacBane, Eliot M. - 98674 E

2. Fitz-Kramer Machines Inc. - 259090   Fitz-Kramer Machines Inc. - 259090
   Marvel Cleaning Service - 482657   Marvel Cleaning Service - 482657
   Donate, Carl G. - 637418   Danato, Carl G. - 687418

3. Martin Davison Trading Corp. - 43108 T   Martin Davidson Trading Corp. - 43108 T
   Cotwald Lighting Fixtures - 76065 L   Cotwald Lighting Fixtures - 70056 L
   R. Crawford Plumbers - 23157 C   R. Crawford Plumbers - 23157 G

4. Fraiman Engineering Corp. - M4773   Friaman Engineering Corp. -M4773
   Neuman, Walter B. - N7745   Neumen, Walter B. - N7745
   Pierce, Eric M. - W6304   Pierce, Eric M. - W6304

5. Constable, Eugene - B 64837   Comstable, Eugene - B 64837
   Derrick, Paul - H 27119   Derrik, Paul - H 27119
   Heller, Karen - S 49606   Heller, Karen - S 46906

6. Hernando Delivery Service Co. - D 7456   Hernando Delivery Service Co. - D 7456
   Barettz Electrical Supplies - N 5392   Barettz Electrical Supplies - N 5392
   Tanner, Abraham - M 4798   Tanner, Abraham - M 4798

7. Kalin Associates - R 38641   Kaline Associates - R 38641
   Sealey, Robert E. - P 63533   Sealey, Robert E. - P 63553
   Scalsi Office Furniture   Scalsi Office Furniture

8. Janowsky, Philip M.- 742213 　　Janowsky, Philip M.- 742213 　　　　　8.____
   Hansen, Thomas H. - 934816 　　Hanson, Thomas H. - 934816
   L. Lester and Son Inc. - 294568 　L. Lester and Son Inc. - 294568

KEY (CORRECT ANSWERS)

1. D
2. C
3. A
4. B
5. A

6. D
7. B
8. C

TEST 4

DIRECTIONS: The following questions are to be answered on the basis of the following Code Table. In this table, for each number, a corresponding code letter is given. Each of the questions contains three pairs of numbers and code letters. In each pair, the code letters should correspond with the numbers in accordance with the Code Table.

CODE TABLE

Number	1	2	3	4	5	6	7	8	9	0
Corresponding Code Letter	Y	N	Z	X	W	T	U	P	S	R

In some of the pairs below, an error exists in the coding. Examine the pairs in each question carefully. If an error exists in:
    Only one of the pairs in the question, mark your answer A.
    Any two pairs in the question, mark your answer B.
    All three pairs in the question, mark your answer C.
    None of the pairs in the question, mark your answer D.

SAMPLE QUESTION

37258   -   ZUNWP
948764   -   SXPTTX
73196   -   UZYSP

In the above sample, the first pair is correct since each number, as listed, has the correct corresponding code letter. In the second pair, an error exists because the number 7 should have the code letter U instead of the letter T. In the third pair, an error exists because the number 6 should have the code letter T instead of the letter P. Since there are errors in two of the three pairs, the correct answer is B.

1.   493785   -   XSZUPW
     86398207   -   PTUSPNRU
     5943162   -   WSXZYTN

2.   5413968412   -   WXYZSTPXYR
     8763451297   -   PUTZXWYZSU
     4781965302   -   XUPYSUWZRN

3.   79137584   -   USYRUWPX
     638247   -   TZPNXS
     49679312   -   XSTUSZYN

4.   37854296   -   ZUPWXNST
     09183298   -   RSYXZNSP
     91762358   -   SYUTNXWP

5.   3918762485   -   ZSYPUTNXPW
     1578291436   -   YWUPNSYXZT
     2791385674   -   NUSYZPWTUX

1.____
2.____
3.____
4.____
5.____

6. 197546821 - YSUWSTPNY   6.____
    873024867 - PUZRNWPTU
    583179246 - WPZYURNXT

7. 510782463 - WYRUSNXTZ   7.____
    478192356 - XUPYSNZWT
    961728532 - STYUNPWXN

KEY (CORRECT ANSWERS)

1. A
2. C
3. B
4. B
5. D

6. C
7. B

TEST 5

DIRECTIONS: Assume that each of the capital letters is the first letter of the name of a city using EAM equipment. The number directly beneath each capital letter is the code number for the city. The small letter beneath each code number is the code letter for the number of EAM divisions in the city and the + or - symbol directly beneath each code letter is the code symbol which signifies whether or not the city uses third generation computers with the EAM equipment.

The questions that follow show City Letters in Column I, Code Numbers in Column II, Code Letters in Column III, and Code Symbols in Column IV. If correct. each City Letter in Column I should correspond by position with each of the three codes shown in the other three columns, in accordance with the coding key shown. BUT there are some errors. For each question,

If there is a total of ONE error in Columns 2, 3, and 4, mark your answer A.
If there is a total of TWO errors in Columns 2, 3, and 4, mark your answer B.
If there is a total of THREE errors in Columns 2, 3, and 4, mark your answer C.
If Columns 2, 3, and 4 are correct, mark your answer D.

SAMPLE QUESTION

I	II	III	IV
City Letter	Code Numbers	Code Letters	Code Symbols
Y J M O S	5 3 7 9 8	e b g i h	- - + + -

The errors are as follows: In Column 2, the Code Number should be "2" instead of "3" for City Letter "J," and in Column 4 the Code Symbol should be "+" instead of "-" for City Letter "Y." Since there is a total of two errors in Columns 2, 3, and 4, the answer to this sample question is B.

Now answer questions 1 through 9 according to these rules.

CODING KEY

City Letter	P J R T Y K M S O
Code Number	1 2 3 4 5 6 7 8 9
Code Letter	a b c d e f g h i
Code Symbol	+ - + - + - + - +

	I City Letters	II Code Numbers	III Code Letters	IV Code Symbols	
1.	K O R M P	6 9 3 7 1	f i e g a	- - + + +	1.____
2.	O T P S Y	9 4 1 8 6	b d a h e	+ - - - +	2.____
3.	R S J T M	3 8 1 4 7	c h b e g	- - - - +	3.____
4.	P M S K J	1 7 8 6 2	a g h f b	+ + - - -	4.____
5.	M Y T J R	7 5 4 2 3	g e d f c	+ + - - +	5.____
6.	T P K Y O	4 1 6 7 9	d a f e i	- + - + -	6.____
7.	S K O R T	8 6 9 3 5	h f i c d	- - + + -	7.____
8.	J R Y P K	2 3 5 1 9	b d e a f	- + + + -	8.____
9.	R O M P Y	4 9 7 1 5	c i g a d	+ + - + +	9.____

KEY (CORRECT ANSWERS)

1. B
2. C
3. C
4. D
5. A

6. B
7. A
8. B
9. C

TEST 6

Assume that each of the capital letters is the first letter of the name of an offense, that the small letter directly beneath each capital letter is the code letter for the offense, and that the number directly beneath each code letter is the file number for the offense.

DIRECTIONS: In each of the following questions, the code letters and file numbers should correspond to the capital letters.

If there is an error only in Column 2, mark your answer A.
If there is an error only in Column 3, mark your answer B.
If there is an error in both Column 2 and Column 3, mark your answer C.
If both Columns 2 and 3 are correct, mark your answer D.

SAMPLE QUESTION

Column 1	Column 2	Column 3
BNARGHSVVU	emoxtylcci	6357905118

The code letters in Column 2 are correct but the first "5" in Column 3 should be "2." Therefore, the answer is B. Now answer the following questions according to the above rules.

CODE TABLE

Name of Offense	V	A	N	D	S	B	R	U	G	H
Code Letter	c	o	m	p	l	e	x	i	t	y
File Number	1	2	3	4	5	6	7	8	9	0

	Column 1	Column 2	Column 3	
1.	HGDSBNBSVR	ytplxmelcx	0945736517	1.____
2.	SDGUUNHVAH	lptiimycoy	5498830120	2.____
3.	BRSNAAVUDU	exlmooctpi	6753221848	3.____
4.	VSRUDNADUS	cleipmopil	1568432485	4.____
5.	NDSHVRBUAG	mplycxeiot	3450175829	5.____
6.	GHUSNVBRDA	tyilmcexpo	9085316742	6.____
7.	DBSHVURANG	pesycixomt	4650187239	7.____
8.	RHNNASBDGU	xymnolepti	7033256398	8.____

KEY (CORRECT ANSWERS)

1. C
2. D
3. A
4. C
5. B

6. D
7. A
8. C

TEST 7

DIRECTIONS: Each of the following questions contains three sets of code letters and code numbers. In each set, the code numbers should correspond with the code letters as given in the Table, but there is a coding error in some of the sets. Examine the sets in each question carefully.

Mark your answer A if there is a coding error in only ONE of the sets in the question.
Mark your answer B if there is a coding error in any TWO of the sets in the question.
Mark your answer C if there is a coding error in all THREE sets in the question.
Mark your answer D if there is a coding error in NONE of the sets in the question.

SAMPLE QUESTION
fgzduwaf - 35720843
uabsdgfw - 04262538
hhfaudgs - 99340257

In the above sample question, the first set is right because each code number matches the code letter as in the Code Table. In the second set, the corresponding number for the code letter b is wrong because it should be 1 instead of 2. In the third set, the corresponding number for the last code letter s is wrong because it should be 6 instead of 7. Since there is an error in two of the sets, the answer to the above sample question is B.

In the Code Table below, each code letter has a corresponding code number directly beneath it.

CODE TABLE

Code Letter	b	d	f	a	g	s	z	w	h	u
Code Number	1	2	3	4	5	6	7	8	9	0

1. fsbughwz - 36104987   zwubgasz - 78025467   1.____
   ghgufddb - 59583221

2. hafgdaas - 94351446   ddsfabsd - 22734162   2.____
   wgdbssgf - 85216553

3. abfbssbd - 41316712   ghzfaubs - 59734017   3.____
   sdbzfwza - 62173874

4. whfbdzag - 89412745   daaszuub - 24467001   4.____
   uzhfwssd - 07936623

5. zbadgbuh - 71425109   dzadbbsz - 27421167   5.____
   gazhwaff - 54798433

6. fbfuadsh - 31304265   gzfuwzsb - 57300671   6.____
   bashhgag - 14699535

2 (#7)

KEY (CORRECT ANSWERS)

1. B
2. C
3. B
4. B
5. D
6. C

TEST 8

DIRECTIONS: The following questions are to be answered on the basis of the following Code Table. In this table every letter has a corresponding code number to be punched. Each question contains three pairs of letters and code numbers. In each pair, the code numbers should correspond with the letters in accordance with the Code Table.

CODE TABLE

Letter	P	L	A	N	D	C	O	B	U	R
Corresponding Code Number	1	2	3	4	5	6	7	8	9	0

In some of the pairs below, an error exists in the coding. Examine the pairs in each question. Mark your answer

A if there is a mistake in only *one* of the pairs
B if there is a mistake in only *two* of the pairs
C if there is a mistake in *all three* of the pairs
D if there is a mistake in *none* of the pairs

SAMPLE QUESTION

LCBPUPAB - 26819138
ACOABOL - 3683872
NDURONUC - 46901496

In the above sample, the first pair is correct since each letter as listed has the correct corresponding code number. In the second pair, an error exists because the letter 0 should have the code number 7, instead of 8. In the third pair, an error exists because the letter D should have the code number 5, instead of 6. Since there are errors in two of the three pairs, your answer should be B.

1. ADCANPLC - 35635126   DORURBBO - 57090877   1.____
   PNACBUCP - 14368061

2. LCOBLRAP - 26782931   UPANUPCD - 91349156   2.____
   RLDACLRO - 02536207

3. LCOROPAR - 26707130   BALANRUP - 83234091   3.____
   DOPOAULL - 57173922

4. ONCRUBAP - 74609831   DCLANORD - 56243705   4.____
   AORPDUR - 3771590

5. PANRBUCD - 13408965   UAOCDPLR - 93765120   5.____
   OPDDOBRA - 71556803

6. BAROLDCP - 83072561   PNOCOBLA - 14767823   6.____
   BURPDOLA - 89015723

7. ANNCPABO - 34461387   DBALDRCP - 58325061   7.____
   ACRPOUL - 3601792

79

2 (#8)

8. BLAPOUR - 8321790 NOACNPL - 4736412 8._____
   RODACORD - 07536805

9. ADUBURCL - 3598062 NOCOBAPR - 47578310 9._____
   PRONDALU - 10754329

10. UBADCLOR - 98356270 NBUPPARA - 48911033 10._____
    LONDUPRC - 27459106

KEY (CORRECT ANSWERS)

1. C
2. B
3. D
4. B
5. A

6. D
7. B
8. B
9. C
10. A

TEST 9

DIRECTIONS: Answer questions 1 through 10 ONLY on the basis of the following information.

Column I consists of serial numbers of dollar bills. Column II shows different ways of arranging the corresponding serial numbers.

The serial numbers of dollar bills in Column I begin and end with a capital letter and have an eight-digit number in between. The serial numbers in Column I are to be arranged according to the following rules:

FIRST: In alphabetical order according to the first letter.

SECOND: When two or more serial numbers have the same first letter, in alphabetical order according to the last letter.

THIRD: When two or more serial numbers have the same first and last letters, in numerical order, beginning with the lowest number.

The serial numbers in Column I are numbered (1) through (5) in the order in which they are listed. In Column II the numbers (1) through (5) are arranged in four different ways to show different arrangements of the corresponding serial numbers. Choose the answer in Column II in which the serial numbers are arranged according to the above rules.

SAMPLE QUESTION

	COLUMN I	COLUMN II
(1)	E75044127B	(A) 4, 1, 3, 2, 5
(2)	B96399104A	(B) 4, 1, 2, 3, 5
(3)	B93939086A	(C) 4, 3, 2, 5, 1
(4)	B47064465H	(D) 3, 2, 5, 4, 1
(5)	B99040922A	

In the sample question, the four serial numbers starting with B should be put before the serial number starting with E. The serial numbers starting with B and ending with A should be put before the serial number starting with B and ending with H. The three serial numbers starting with B and ending with A should be listed in numerical order, beginning with the lowest number. The correct way to arrange the serial numbers, therefore, is:

- (3) B93939086A
- (2) B96399104A
- (5) B99040922A
- (4) B47064465H
- (1) E75044127B

Since the order of arrangement is 3, 2, 5, 4, 1, the answer to the sample question is (D).

		COLUMN I		COLUMN II
1.	(1)	P44343314Y	A.	2, 3, 1, 4, 5
	(2)	P44141341S	B.	1, 5, 3, 2, 4
	(3)	P44141431L	C.	4, 2, 3, 5, 1
	(4)	P41143413W	D.	5, 3, 2, 4, 1
	(5)	P44313433H		
2.	(1)	D89077275M	A.	3, 2, 5, 4, 1
	(2)	D98073724N	B.	1, 4, 3, 2, 5
	(3)	D90877274N	C.	4, 1, 5, 2, 3
	(4)	D98877275M	D.	1, 3, 2, 5, 4
	(5)	D98873725N		

3.	(1)	H32548137E		A.	2,	4,	5,	1,	3
	(2)	H35243178A		B.	1,	5,	2,	3,	4
	(3)	H35284378F		C.	1,	5,	2,	4,	3
	(4)	H35288337A		D.	2,	1,	5,	3,	4
	(5)	H32883173B							
4.	(1)	K24165039H		A.	4,	2,	5,	3,	1
	(2)	F24106599A		B.	2,	3,	4,	1,	5
	(3)	L21406639G		C.	4,	2,	5,	1,	3
	(4)	C24156093A		D.	1,	3,	4,	5,	2
	(5)	K24165593D							
5.	(1)	H79110642E		A.	2,	1,	3,	5,	4
	(2)	H79101928E		B.	2,	1,	4,	5,	3
	(3)	A79111567F		C.	3,	5,	2,	1,	4
	(4)	H79111796E		D.	4,	3,	5,	1,	2
	(5)	A79111618F							
6.	(1)	P16388385W		A.	3,	4,	5,	2,	1
	(2)	R16388335V		B.	2,	3,	4,	5,	1
	(3)	P16383835W		C.	2,	4,	3,	1,	5
	(4)	R18386865V		D.	3,	1,	5,	2,	4
	(5)	P18686865W							
7.	(1)	B42271749G		A.	4,	1,	5,	2,	3
	(2)	B42271779G		B.	4,	1,	2,	5,	3
	(3)	E43217779G		C.	1,	2,	4,	5,	3
	(4)	B42874119C		D.	5,	3,	1,	2,	4
	(5)	E42817749G							
8.	(1)	M57906455S		A.	4,	1,	5,	3,	2
	(2)	N87077758S		B.	3,	4,	1,	5,	2
	(3)	N87707757B		C.	4,	1,	5,	2,	3
	(4)	M57877759B		D.	1,	5,	3,	2,	4
	(5)	M57906555S							
9.	(1)	C69336894Y		A.	2,	5,	3,	1,	4
	(2)	C69336684V		B.	3,	2,	5,	1,	4
	(3)	C69366887W		C.	3,	1,	4,	5,	2
	(4)	C69366994Y		D.	2,	5,	1,	3,	4
	(5)	C69336865V							
10.	(1)	A56247181D		A.	1,	5,	3,	2,	4
	(2)	A56272128P		B.	3,	1,	5,	2,	4
	(3)	H56247128D		C.	3,	2,	1,	5,	4
	(4)	H56272288P		D.	1,	5,	2,	3,	4
	(5)	A56247188D							

KEY (CORRECT ANSWERS)

1.	D		6.	D
2.	B		7.	B
3.	A		8.	A
4.	C		9.	A
5.	C		10.	D

TEST 10

DIRECTIONS: Answer the following questions on the basis of the instructions, the code, and the sample questions given below. Assume that an officer at a certain location is equipped with a two-way radio to keep him in constant touch with his security headquarters. Radio messages and replies are given in code form, as follows:

CODE TABLE

	J	P	M	F	B
Radio Code for Situation					
Radio Code for Action to be Taken	o	r	a	z	q
Radio Response for Action Being Taken	1	2	3	4	5

Assume that each of the above capital letters is the radio code for a particular type of situation, that the small letter below each capital letter is the radio code for the action an officer is directed to take, and that the number directly below each small letter is the radio response an officer should make to indicate what action was actually taken.

In each of the following questions, the code letter for the action directed (Column 2) and the code number for the action taken (Column 3) should correspond to the capital letters in Column 1.

INSTRUCTIONS: If only Column 2 is different from Column 1, mark your answer I.
If only Column 3 is different from Column 1, mark your answer II.
If both Column 2 and Column 3 are different from Column I, mark your answer III.
If both Columns 2 and 3 are the same as Column 1, mark your answer IV.

SAMPLE QUESTION

Column 1	Column 2	Column 3
JPFMB	orzaq	12453

The CORRECT answer is: A. I B. II C. III D. IV

The code letters in Column 2 are correct, but the numbers "53" in Column 3 should be "35." Therefore, the answer is B. Now answe the following questions according to the above rules.

	Column 1	Column 2	Column 3	
1.	PBFJM	rqzoa	25413	1.____
2.	MPFBJ	zrqao	32541	2.____
3.	JBFPM	oqzra	15432	3.____
4.	BJPMF	qaroz	51234	4.____
5.	PJFMB	rozaq	21435	5.____
6.	FJBMP	zoqra	41532	6.____

KEY (CORRECT ANSWERS)

1. D
2. C
3. B
4. A
5. D
6. A

ARITHMETIC
EXAMINATION SECTION

DIRECTIONS: Each question or incomplete statement is followed by several suggested answers or completions. Select the one that BEST answers the question or completes the statement. *PRINT THE LETTER OF THE CORRECT ANSWER IN THE SPACE AT THE RIGHT.*

1. The sum of 53632 + 27403 + 98765 + 75424 is   1.____
   A. 19214   B. 215214   C. 235224   D. 255224

2. The sum of 76342 + 49050 + 21206 + 59989 is   2.____
   A. 196586   B. 206087   C. 206587   D. 234487

3. The sum of $452.13 + $963.45 + $621.25 is   3.____
   A. $1936.83   B. $2036.83   C. $2095.73   D. $2135.73

4. The sum of 36392 + 42156 + 98765 is   4.____
   A. 167214   B. 177203   C. 177313   D. 178213

5. The sum of 40125 + 87123 + 24689 is   5.____
   A. 141827   B. 151827   C. 151937   D. 161947

6. The sum of 2379 + 4015 + 6521 + 9986 is   6.____
   A. 22901   B. 22819   C. 21801   D. 21791

7. From 50962 subtract 36197.
   The answer should be   7.____
   A. 14675   B. 14765   C. 14865   D. 24765

8. From 90000 subtract 31928.
   The answer should be   8.____
   A. 58072   B. 59062   C. 68172   D. 69182

9. From 63764 subtract 21548.
   The answer should be   9.____
   A. 42216   B. 43122   C. 45126   D. 85312

10. From $9605.13 subtract $2715.96.
    The answer should be   10.____
    A. $12,321.09   B. $8,690.16   C. $6,990.07   D. $6,889.17

11. From 76421 subtract 73101.
    The answer should be   11.____
    A. 3642   B. 3540   C. 3320   D. 3242

12. From $8.25 subtract $6.50.
    The answer should be
    A. $1.25   B. $1.50   C. $1.75   D. $2.25

13. Multiply 563 by 0.50.
    The answer should be
    A. 281.50   B. 28.15   C. 2.815   D. 0.2815

14. Multiply 0.35 by 1045.
    The answer should be
    A. 0.36575   B. 3.6575   C. 36.575   D. 365.75

15. Multiply 25 by 2513.
    The answer should be
    A. 62825   B. 62725   C. 60825   D. 52825

16. Multiply 423 by 0.01.
    The answer should be
    A. 0.0423   B. 0.423   C. 4.23   D. 42.3

17. Multiply 6.70 by 3.2.
    The answer should be
    A. 2.1440   B. 21.440   C. 214.40   D. 2144.0

18. Multiply 630 by 517.
    The answer should be
    A. 325,710   B. 345,720   C. 362,425   D. 385,660

19. Multiply 35 by 846.
    The answer should be
    A. 4050   B. 9450   C. 18740   D. 29610

20. Multiply 823 by 0.05.
    The answer should be
    A. 0.4115   B. 4.115   C. 41.15   D. 411.50

21. Multiply 1690 by 0.10.
    The answer should be
    A. 0.169   B. 1.69   C. 16.90   D. 169.0

22. Divide 2765 by 35.
    The answer should be
    A. 71   B. 79   C. 87   D. 93

23. From $18.55 subtract $6.80.
    The answer should be
    A. $9.75   B. $10.95   C. $11.75   D. $25.35

24. The sum of 2.75 + 4.50 + 3.60 is 24._____
   A. 9.75   B. 10.85   C. 11.15   D. 11.95

25. The sum of 9.63 + 11.21 + 17.25 is 25._____
   A. 36.09   B. 38.09   C. 39.92   D. 41.22

26. The sum of 112.0 + 16.9 + 3.84 is 26._____
   A. 129.3   B. 132.74   C. 136.48   D. 167.3

27. When 65 is added to the result of 14 multiplied by 13, the answer is 27._____
   A. 92   B. 182   C. 247   D. 16055

28. From $391.55 subtract $273.45. 28._____
   The answer should be
   A. $118.10   B. $128.20   C. $178.10   D. $218.20

29. When 119 is subtracted from the sum of 2016 + 1634, the answer is 29._____
   A. 2460   B. 3531   C. 3650   D. 3769

30. What is $367.20 + $510.00 + $402.80? 30._____
   A. $1,276.90   B. $1,277.90   C. $1,279.00   D. $1,280.00

31. Multiply 35 x 65 x 15. 31._____
   The answer should be
   A. 2275   B. 24265   C. 31145   D. 34125

32. Multiply 40 x 65 x 10. 32._____
   The answer should be
   A. 26000   B. 28000   C. 25200   D. 22300

33. The total amount of money represented by 43 half-dollars, 26 quarters, and 71 dimes is 33._____
   A. $28.00   B. $35.10   C. $44.30   D. $56.60

34. The total amount of money represented by 132 quarters, 97 dimes, and 220 nickels is 34._____
   A. $43.70   B. $44.20   C. $52.90   D. $53.70

35. The total amount of money represented by 40 quarters, 40 dimes, and 20 nickels is 35._____
   A. $14.50   B. $15.00   C. $15.50   D. $16.00

36. The sum of $29.61 + $101.53 + $943.64 is 36._____
   A. $983.88   B. $1074.78   C. $1174.98   D. $1341.42

37. The sum of $132.25 + $85.63 + $7056.44 is 37._____
   A. $1694.19   B. $7274.32   C. $8464.57   D. $9346.22

38. The sum of 4010 + 1271 + 23 + 838 is   38._____

   A. 6142   B. 6162   C. 6242   D. 6362

39. What is the value of 3 twenty dollar bills, 5 ten dollar bills, 13 five dollar bills, and 43 one   39._____
    dollar bills?

   A. $218.00   B. $219.00   C. $220.00   D. $221.00

40. What is the value of 8 twenty dollar bills, 13 ten dollar bills, 27 five dollar bills, 3 two dollar   40._____
    bills, and 43 one dollar bills?

   A. $364.00   B. $374.00   C. $474.00   D. $485.00

41. What is the value of 6 twenty dollar bills, 8 ten dollar bills, 19 five dollar bills, and 37 one   41._____
    dollar bills?

   A. $232.00   B. $233.00   C. $332.00   D. $333.00

42. What is the value of 13 twenty dollar bills, 17 ten dollar bills, 24 five dollar bills, 7 two dol-   42._____
    lar bills, and 55 one dollar bills?

   A. $594.00   B. $599.00   C. $609.00   D. $619.00

43. What is the value of 7 half dollars, 9 quarters, 23 dimes, and 17 nickels?   43._____

   A. $7.80   B. $7.90   C. $8.80   D. $8.90

44. What is the value of 3 one dollar coins, 3 half dollars, 7 quarters, 13 dimes, and 27 nick-   44._____
    els?

   A. $7.80   B. $8.70   C. $8.80   D. $8.90

45. What is the value of 73 quarters?   45._____

   A. $18.25   B. $18.50   C. $18.75   D. $19.00

46. What is the value of 173 nickels?   46._____

   A. $8.55   B. $8.65   C. $8.75   D. $8.85

47. In checking a book of consecutively numbered Senior Citizen tickets, you find there are   47._____
    no tickets between number 13,383 and 13,833.
    How many tickets are missing?

   A. 448   B. 449   C. 450   D. 451

48. A ticket clerk begins her shift with 2,322 tickets. How many tickets will she have at the   48._____
    end of her shift if she sells 1,315 and collects 1,704 from the turnstiles during her shift?

   A. 2,687   B. 2,693   C. 2,711   D. 2,722

49. A ticket clerk has three books of tickets. One contains 273 tickets, one contains 342 tick-   49._____
    ets, and one contains 159 tickets. The clerk combines the contents of the three books
    and then sells 217 tickets.
    How many tickets are left?

   A. 556   B. 557   C. 568   D. 991

50. A ticket clerk has a quantity of consecutively numbered tickets. The number on the ticket having the lowest number is 27,069. The number on the ticket having the highest number is 27,154.
How many tickets does the clerk have?

   A. 84   B. 85   C. 86   D. 87

50.____

KEY (CORRECT ANSWERS)

1. D	11. C	21. D	31. D	41. C
2. C	12. C	22. B	32. A	42. D
3. B	13. A	23. C	33. B	43. D
4. C	14. D	24. B	34. D	44. D
5. C	15. A	25. B	35. B	45. A
6. A	16. C	26. B	36. B	46. B
7. B	17. B	27. C	37. B	47. B
8. A	18. A	28. A	38. A	48. C
9. A	19. D	29. B	39. A	49. B
10. D	20. C	30. D	40. C	50. C

6 (#1)

SOLUTIONS TO PROBLEMS

1. 53,632 + 27,403 + 98,765 + 75,424 = 255,224

2. 76,342 + 49,050 + 21,206 + 59,989 = 206,587

3. $452.13 + $963.83 + $621.25 = $2037.21

4. 36,392 + 42,156 + 98,765 = 177,313

5. 40,125 + 87,123 + 24,689 = 151,937

6. 2379 + 4015 + 6521 + 9986 = 22901

7. 50,962 - 36,197 = 14,765

8. 90,000 - 31,928 = 58,072

9. 63,764 - 21,548 = 42,216

10. $9605.13 - $2715.96 = $6889.17

11. 76,421 - 73,101 = 3320

12. $8.25 - $6.50 = $1.75

13. (563)(.50) = 281.50

14. (.35)(1045) = 365.75

15. (25)(2513) = 62,825

16. (423)(.01) = 4.23

17. (6.70)(3.2) = 21.44

18. (630)(517) = 325,710

19. (35)(846) = 29,610

20. (823)(.05) = 41.15

21. (1690)(.10) = 169

22. 2765 / 35 = 79

23. $18.55 - $6.80 = $11.75

24. 2.75 + 4.50 + 3.60 = 10.85

25. 9.63 + 11.21 + 17.25 = 38.09

26. 112.0 + 16.9 + 3.84 = 132.74

27. 65 + (14)(13) = 247

28. $391.55 - $273.45 = $118.10

29. 2016 + 1634 - 119 = 3531

30. $367.20 + $510.00 + $402.80 = $1280.00

31. (35)(65)(15) = 34,125

32. (40)(65)(10) - 26,000

33. (43)(.50) + (26)(.25) + (71)(.10) = $35.10

34. (132)(.25) + (97)(.10) + (220)(.05) = $53.70

35. (40)(.25) + (40)(.10) + (20)(.05) = $15.00

36. $29.61 + $101.53 + $943.64 = $1074.78

37. $132.25 + $85.63 + $7056.44 = $7274.32

38. 4010 + 1271 + 23 + 838 = 6142

39. (3)($20) + (5)($10) + (13)($5) + (43)($1) + $218.00

40. (8)($20) + (13)($10) + (27)($5) + (3)($2) + (43)($1) = $474.00

41. (6)($20) + (8)($10) + (19)($5) + (37)($1) = $332.00

42. (13)($20) + (17)($10) + (24)($5) + (7)($2) + (55)($1) = $619.00

43. (7)(.50) + (9)(.25) + (23)(.10) + (17)(.05) = $8.90

44. (3)($1) + (3)(.50) + (7)(.25) + (13)(.10) + (27)(.05) = $8.90

45. (73)(.25) = $18.25

46. (173)(.05) = $8.65

47. The missing tickets are numbered 13,384 through 13,832. This represents 13,832 - 13,384 + 1 = 449 tickets.

48. 2322 - 1315 + 1704 = 2711 tickets left.

49. 273 + 342 + 159 - 217 = 557 tickets left

50. 27,154 - 27,069 + 1 = 86 tickets

ARITHMETIC

EXAMINATION SECTION
TEST 1

DIRECTIONS: Each question or incomplete statement is followed by several suggested answers or completions. Select the one that BEST answers the question or completes the statement. *PRINT THE LETTER OF THE CORRECT ANSWER IN THE SPACE AT THE RIGHT.*

1. The sum of 76342 + 49050 + 21206 + 59989 is
    A. 196586   B. 206087   C. 206587   D. 234487

2. The sum of $452.13 + $963.83 + $621.25 is
    A. $1936.83   B. $2037.21   C. $2095.73   D. $2135.73

3. The sum of 36392 + 42156 + 98765 is
    A. 167214   B. 177203   C. 177313   D. 178213

4. The sum of 40125 + 87123 + 24689 is
    A. 141827   B. 151827   C. 151937   D. 161947

5. The sum of 2379 + 4015 + 6521 + 9986 is
    A. 22901   B. 22819   C. 21801   D. 21791

6. From 50962 subtract 36197. The answer should be
    A. 14675   B. 14765   C. 14865   D. 24765

7. From 90000 subtract 31928. The answer should be
    A. 58072   B. 59062   C. 68172   D. 69182

8. From 63764 subtract 21548. The answer should be
    A. 42216   B. 43122   C. 45126   D. 85312

9. From $9605.13 subtract $2715.96. The answer should be
    A. $12,321.09   B. $8,690.16
    C. $6,990.07   D. $6,889.17

10. From 76421 subtract 73101. The answer should be
    A. 3642   B. 3540   C. 3320   D. 3242

11. From $8.25 subtract $6.50. The answer should be
    A. $1.25   B. $1.50   C. $1.75   D. $2.25

12. Multiply 563 by 0.50. The answer should be
    A. 281.50   B. 28.15   C. 2.815   D. 0.2815

13. Multiply 0.35 by 1045. The answer should be
    A. 0.36575   B. 3.6575   C. 36.575   D. 365.75

14. Multiply 25 by 2513. The answer should be
    A. 62825   B. 62725   C. 60825   D. 52825

15. Multiply 423 by 0.01. The answer should be
    A. 0.0423   B. 0.423   C. 4.23   D. 42.3

16. Multiply 6.70 by 3.2. The answer should be
    A. 2.1440   B. 21.440   C. 214.40   D. 2144.0

17. Multiply 630 by 517. The answer should be
    A. 325,710   B. 345,720   C. 362,425   D. 385,660

18. Multiply 35 by 846. The answer should be
    A. 4050   B. 9450   C. 18740   D. 29610

19. Multiply 823 by 0.05. The answer should be
    A. 0.4115   B. 4.115   C. 41.15   D. 411.50

20. Multiply 1690 by 0.10. The answer should be
    A. 0.169   B. 1.69   C. 16.90   D. 169.0

21. Divide 2765 by 35. The answer should be
    A. 71   B. 79   C. 87   D. 93

22. From $18.55 subtract $6.80. The answer should be
    A. $9.75   B. $10.95   C. $11.75   D. $25.35

23. The sum of 2.75 + 4.50 + 3.60 is
    A. 9.75   B. 10.85   C. 11.15   D. 11.95

24. The sum of 9.63 + 11.21 + 17.25 is
    A. 36.09   B. 38.09   C. 39.92   D. 41.22

25. The sum of 112.0 + 16.9 + 3.84 is
    A. 129.3   B. 132.74   C. 136.48   D. 167.3

KEY (CORRECT ANSWERS)

1. C		11. C
2. B		12. A
3. C		13. D
4. C		14. A
5. A		15. C
6. B		16. B
7. A		17. A
8. A		18. D
9. D		19. C
10. C		20. D

21. B
22. C
23. B
24. B
25. B

4 (#1)

SOLUTIONS TO PROBLEMS

1. 76,342 + 49,050 + 21,206 + 59,989 = 206,587
2. $452.13 + $963.83 + $621.25 = $2037.21
3. 36,392 + 42,156 + 98,765 = 177,313
4. 40,125 + 87,123 + 24,689 = 151,937
5. 2379 + 4015 + 6521 + 9986 = 22901
6. 50,962 - 36,197 = 14,765
7. 90,000 - 31,928 = 58,072
8. 63,764 - 21,548 = 42,216
9. $9605.13 - $2715.96 = $6889.17
10. 76,421 - 73,101 = 3320
11. $8.25 - $6.50 = $1.75
12. (563)(.50) = 281.50
13. (.35)(1045) = 365.75
14. (25)(2513) = 62,825
15. (423)(.01) = 4.23
16. (6.70)(3.2) = 21.44
17. (630)(517) = 325,710
18. (35)(846) = 29,610
19. (823)(.05) = 41.15
20. (1690)(.10) = 169
21. 2765 ÷ 35 = 79
22. $18.55 - $6.80 = $11.75
23. 2.75 + 4.50 + 3.60 = 10.85
24. 9.63 + 11.21 + 17.25 = 38.09
25. 112.0 + 16.9 + 3.84 = 132.74

TEST 2

Questions 1-10.

DIRECTIONS: Questions 1 through 10 refer to the arithmetic examples shown in the boxes below. Be sure to refer to the proper box when answering each question.

23.3 - 5.72	$491.26 -127.47	$7.95 ÷ $0.15	4758 1639 2075 864 23	27.6 179.47 8.73 46.5
BOX 1	BOX 2	BOX 3	BOX 4	BOX 5
243 x57	57697 -9748	23.65 x 9.7	3/4 260	25/1975
BOX 6	BOX 7	BOX 8	BOX 9	BOX 10

1. The difference between the two numbers in Box 1 is

    A. 17.42   B. 17.58   C. 23.35   D. 29.02

2. The difference between the two numbers in Box 2 is

    A. $274.73   B. $363.79   C. $374.89   D. $618.73

3. The result of the division indicated in Box 3 is

    A. $0.53   B. $5.30   C. 5.3   D. 53

4. The sum of the five numbers in Box 4 is

    A. 8355   B. 9359   C. 9534   D. 10359

5. The sum of the four numbers in Box 5 is

    A. 262.30   B. 272.03   C. 372.23   D. 372.30

6. The product of the two numbers in Box 6 is

    A. 138.51   B. 1385.1   C. 13851   D. 138510

7. The difference between the two numbers in Box 7 is

    A. 67445   B. 48949   C. 47949   D. 40945

8. The product of the two numbers in Box 8 is

    A. 22.9405   B. 229.405   C. 2294.05   D. 229405

9. The product of the two numbers in Box 9 is

    A. 65   B. 120   C. 195   D. 240

10. The result of the division indicated in Box 10 is

    A. 790   B. 379   C. 179   D. 79

Questions 11-20.

DIRECTIONS: Questions 11 through 20 refer to the arithmetic examples shown in the boxes below. Be sure to refer to the proper box when answering each question.

3849 728 3164 773 32	18.70 268.38 17.64 9.40	66788 -8639	154 x48	32.56 x 8.6
BOX 1	BOX 2	BOX 3	BOX 4	BOX 5
34/2890	32.49 - 8.7	$582.17 -38.58	$6.72 ÷ $0.24	3/8 x 264
BOX 6	BOX 7	BOX 8	BOX 9	BOX 10

11. The sum of the five numbers in Box 1 is

    A. 7465   B. 7566   C. 8465   D. 8546

12. The sum of the four numbers in Box 2 is

    A. 341.21   B. 341.12   C. 314.21   D. 314.12

13. The difference between the two numbers in Box 3 is

    A. 75427   B. 74527   C. 58149   D. 57149

14. The product of the two numbers in Box 4 is

    A. 1232   B. 6160   C. 7392   D. 8392

15. The product of the two numbers in Box 5 is

    A. 28.016   B. 280.016   C. 280.16   D. 2800.16

16. The result of the division indicated in Box 6 is

    A. 85   B. 850   C. 8.5   D. 185

17. The difference between the two numbers in Box 7 is

    A. 23.79   B. 21.53   C. 19.97   D. 18.79

18. The difference between the two numbers in Box 8 is

    A. $620.75   B. $602.59   C. $554.75   D. $543.59

19. The result of the division indicated in Box 9 is

    A. .0357   B. 28.0   C. 280   D. 35.7

20. The product of the two numbers in Box 10 is 20._____
    A. 9.90 B. 89.0 C. 99.0 D. 199.

21. When 2597 is added to the result of 257 multiplied by 65, the answer is 21._____
    A. 16705 B. 19302 C. 19392 D. 19402

22. When 948 is subtracted from the sum of 6527 + 324, the answer is 22._____
    A. 5255 B. 5903 C. 7151 D. 7799

23. When 736 is subtracted from the sum of 3191 + 1253, the answer is 23._____
    A. 2674 B. 3708 C. 4444 D. 5180

24. Divide 6 2/3 by 2 1/2. 24._____
    A. 2 2/3 B. 16 2/3 C. 3 1/3 D. 2 1/2

25. Add: 1/2 + 2 1/4 + 2/3 25._____
    A. 3 1/4 B. 2 7/8 C. 4 1/4 D. 3 5/12

KEY (CORRECT ANSWERS)

1. B
2. B
3. D
4. B
5. A

6. C
7. C
8. B
9. C
10. D

11. D
12. D
13. C
14. C
15. B

16. A
17. A
18. D
19. B
20. C

21. B
22. B
23. B
24. A
25. D

4 (#2)

SOLUTIONS TO PROBLEMS

1. 23.3 - 5.72 = 17.58

2. $491.26 - $127.47 = $363.79

3. $7.95 $.15 = 53

4. 4758 + 1639 + 2075 + 864 + 23 = 9359

5. 27.6 + 179.47 + 8.73 + 46.5 = 262.3

6. (243)(57) = 13,851

7. 57,697 - 9748 = 47,949

8. (23.65X9.7) = 229.405

9. $(\frac{3}{4})(260) = 195$

10. 1975 ÷ 25 = 79

11. 3849 + 728 + 3164 + 773 + 32 = 8546

12. 18.70 + 268.38 + 17.64 + 9.40 = 314.12

13. 66,788 - 8639 = 58,149

14. (154)(48) = 7392

15. (32.56)(8.6) = 280.016

16. 2890 34 = 85

17. 32.49 - 8.7 = 23.79

18. $582.17 - $38.58 = $543.59

19. $6.72 ÷ $.24 = 28

20. $(\frac{3}{8})(264) = 99$

21. 2597 + (257)(65) = 2597 + 16,705 = 19,302

22. (6527 + 324) - 948 = 6851 - 948 = 5903

23. (3191 + 1253) - 736 = 4444 - 736 = 3708

24. $6\frac{2}{3} \div 2\frac{1}{2} = (\frac{20}{3})(\frac{2}{5}) = \frac{40}{15} = 2\frac{2}{3}$

25. $\frac{1}{2} + 2\frac{1}{4} + \frac{2}{3} = \frac{6}{12} + 2\frac{3}{12} + \frac{8}{12} = 2\frac{17}{12} = 3\frac{5}{12}$

TEST 3

Questions 1-10.

DIRECTIONS: Questions 1 through 10 refer to the arithmetic examples shown in the boxes below. Be sure to refer to the proper box when answering each item.

8462 2974 5109 763 47 BOX 1	14/1890 BOX 2	182 x63 BOX 3	27412 -8426 BOX 4	$275.15 -162.28 BOX 5
2/3 x 246 BOX 6	14.36 x 7.2 BOX 7	14.6 9.22 143.18 27.1 BOX 8	$6.45 ÷ $0.15 BOX 9	16.6 - 7.91 BOX 10

1. The sum of the five numbers in Box 1 is   1._____
   A. 16245   B. 16355   C. 17245   D. 17355

2. The result of the division indicated in Box 2 is   2._____
   A. 140   B. 135   C. 127 6/7   D. 125

3. The product of the two numbers in Box 3 is   3._____
   A. 55692   B. 16552   C. 11466   D. 1638

4. The difference between the two numbers in Box 4 is   4._____
   A. 18986   B. 19096   C. 35838   D. 38986

5. The difference between the two numbers in Box 5 is   5._____
   A. $103.87   B. $112.87   C. $113.97   D. $212.87

6. The product of the two numbers in Box 6 is   6._____
   A. 82   B. 123   C. 164   D. 369

7. The product of the two numbers in Box 7 is   7._____
   A. 103.492   B. 103.392   C. 102.392   D. 102.292

8. The sum of the four numbers in Box 8 is   8._____
   A. 183.00   B. 183.10   C. 194.10   D. 204.00

9. The result of the division indicated in Box 9 is   9._____
   A. $0.43   B. 4.3   C. 43   D. $4.30

10. The difference between the two numbers in Box 10 is
    A. 8.69   B. 8.11   C. 6.25   D. 3.75

11. Add $4.34, $34.50, $6.00, $101.76, and $90.67. From the result, subtract $60.54 and $10.56.
    A. $76.17   B. $156.37   C. $166.17   D. $300.37

12. Add 2,200, 2,600, 252, and 47.96. From the result, subtract 202.70, 1,200, 2,150, and 434.43.
    A. 1,112.83   B. 1,213.46   C. 1,341.51   D. 1,348.91

13. Multiply 1850 by .05 and multiply 3300 by .08. Then, add both results.
    A. 242.50   B. 264.00   C. 333.25   D. 356.50

14. Multiply 312.77 by .04. Round off the result to the nearest hundredth.
    A. 12.52   B. 12.511   C. 12.518   D. 12.51

15. Add 362.05, 91.13, 347.81, and 17.46. Then, divide the result by 6. The answer rounded off to the nearest hundredth is
    A. 138.409   B. 137.409   C. 136.41   D. 136.40

16. Add 66.25 and 15.06. Then, multiply the result by 2 1/6. The answer is MOST NEARLY
    A. 176.18   B. 176.17   C. 162.66   D. 162.62

17. Each of the following options contains three decimals. In which case do all three decimals have the same value?
    A. .3; .30; .03
    B. .25; .250; .2500
    C. 1.9; 1.90; 1.09
    D. .35; .350; .035

18. Add 1/2 the sum of (539.84 and 479.26) to 1/3 the sum of (1461.93 and 927.27). Round off the result to the nearest whole number.
    A. 3408   B. 2899   C. 1816   D. 1306

19. Multiply $5,906.09 by 15%. Then, divide the result by 3.
    A. $295.30   B. $885.91   C. $8,859.14   D. $29,530.45

20. A team has won 10 games, lost 4, and has 6 games yet to play. How many of these remaining games MUST be won if the team is to win 65% of its games for the season?
    A. One
    B. Two
    C. Four
    D. None of the above

21. If a certain candy sells at the rate of $1 for 2 1/2 ounces, what is the price per pound? (Do not include tax.)
    A. $2.50   B. $6.40   C. $8.50   D. $4.00

22. Which is the SMALLEST of the following numbers? 22.____

   A. .3980 B. .3976 C. .39752 D. .399

23. A tank can be filled by one pipe in 10 minutes and by another in 15 minutes. How long will it take to fill the tank if both pipes are opened? _____ min. 23.____

   A. 4 B. 5 C. 6 D. 7.5

24. If $17.60 is to be divided between two people so that one person receives one and three-fourths as much as the other, how much should each receive? 24.____

   A. $6.40 and $11.20
   B. $5.50 and $12.10
   C. $6.60 and $11.20
   D. $6.00 and $11.60

25. Mr. Burns owns a block of land which is exactly 320 ft. long and 140 ft. wide. At 40¢ per square foot, how much will it cost to build a 4 foot cement walk around this land, bound by its outer edge? 25.____

   A. $1420.80 B. $1472 C. $368 D. $1446.40

KEY (CORRECT ANSWERS)

1. D		11. C	
2. B		12. A	
3. C		13. D	
4. A		14. D	
5. B		15. C	
6. C		16. B	
7. B		17. B	
8. C		18. D	
9. C		19. A	
10. A		20. D	

21. B
22. C
23. C
24. A
25. D

SOLUTIONS TO PROBLEMS

1. $8462 + 2974 + 5109 + 763 + 47 = 17{,}355$

2. $1890 \div 14 = 135$

3. $(182)(63) = 11{,}466$

4. $27{,}412 - 8426 = 18{,}986$

5. $\$275.15 - \$162.28 = \$112.87$

6. $(\frac{2}{3})(246) = 164$

7. $(14.36)(7.2) = 103.392$

8. $14.6 + 9.22 + 143.18 + 27.1 = 194.1$

9. $\$6.45\ \$.15 = 43$

10. $16.6 - 7.91 = 8.69$

11. $(\$4.34 + \$34.50 + \$6.00 + \$101.76 + \$90.67) - (\$60.54 + \$10.56) = \$237.27 - \$71.10 = \$166.17$

12. $(2200 + 2600 + 252 + 47.96) - (202.70 + 1200 + 2150 + 434.43) = 5099.96 - 3987.13 = 1112.83$

13. $(1850)(.05) + (3300 \times .08) = 92.5 + 264 = 356.5$

14. $(312.77)(.04) = 12.5108 = 12.51$ rounded off to nearest hundredth

15. $(362.05 + 91.13 + 347.81 + 17.46)\ 6 = 818.45\ 6 = 136.4083" = 136.41$ rounded off to nearest hundredth

16. $(66.25 + 15.06)(2\frac{1}{6}) = (81.31)(2\frac{1}{6}) \approx 176.17$

17. $.25 = .250 = .2500$

18. $1/2(539.84 + 479.26) + 1/3(1461.93 + 927.27) = 509.55 + 796.4 = 1305.95 = 1306$ rounaed off to nearest whole number

19. $(\$5906.09)(.15)(\frac{1}{3}) = \$295.3045 = \$295.30$ rounded off to 2 places

5 (#3)

20. (.65)(20) = 13 games won. Thus, the team must win 3 more games.

21. Let x = price per pound. Then, $\dfrac{1.00}{x} = \dfrac{2\frac{1}{2}}{16}$. Solving, x = 6.40

22. .39752 is the smallest of the numbers.

23. Let x = required minutes. Then, $\dfrac{x}{10} + \dfrac{x}{15} = 1$. So, 3x + 2x = 30. Solving, x = 6.

24. Let x, 1.75x represent the two amounts. Then, x + 1.75x = $17.60. Solving, x = $6.40 and 1.75x = $11.20.

25. Area of cement walk = (320)(140) - (312)(132) = 3616 sq.ft. Then, (3616)(.40) = $1446.40.

TEST 4

DIRECTIONS: Each question or incomplete statement is followed by several suggested answers or completions. Select the one that BEST answers the question or completes the statement. *PRINT THE LETTER OF THE CORRECT ANSWER IN THE SPACE AT THE RIGHT.*

1. Subtract: 10,376
   -8,492

   A. 1834   B. 1884   C. 1924   D. 2084

   1.____

2. Subtract: $155.22
   - 93.75

   A. $61.47   B. $59.33   C. $59.17   D. $58.53

   2.____

3. Subtract: $22.50
   -13.78

   A. $9.32   B. $9.18   C. $8.92   D. $8.72

   3.____

4. Multiply: 485
   x32

   A. 13,350   B. 15,520   C. 16,510   D. 17,630

   4.____

5. Multiply: $3.29
   x 14

   A. $41.16   B. $42.46   C. $44.76   D. $46.06

   5.____

6. Multiply: 106
   x318

   A. 33,708   B. 33,632   C. 33,614   D. 33,548

   6.____

7. Multiply: 119
   x1.15

   A. 136.85   B. 136.94   C. 137.15   D. 137.34

   7.____

8. Divide: 432 by 16

   A. 37   B. 32   C. 27   D. 24

   8.____

9. Divide: $115.65 by 5

   A. $24.25   B. $23.13   C. $22.83   D. $22.55

   9.____

10. Divide: 18,711 by 63

    A. 267   B. 273   C. 283   D. 297

    10.____

11. Divide: 327.45 by .15

    A. 1,218   B. 2,183   C. 2,243   D. 2,285

    11.____

12. The sum of 637.894, 8352.16, 4.8673, and 301.5 is MOST NEARLY

    A. 8989.5   B. 9021.35   C. 9294.9   D. 9296.4

13. If 30 is divided by .06, the result is

    A. 5   B. 50   C. 500   D. 5000

14. The sum of the fractions 1/3, 4/6, 3/4, 1/2, and 1/12 is

    A. 3 1/4   B. 2 1/3   C. 2 1/6   D. 1 11/12

15. If 96934.42 is divided by 53.496, the result is MOST NEARLY

    A. 181   B. 552   C. 1812   D. 5520

16. If 25% of a number is 48, the number is

    A. 12   B. 60   C. 144   D. 192

17. The average number of reports filed per day by a clerk during a five-day week was 720. He filed 610 reports the first day, 720 reports the second day, 740 reports the third day, and 755 reports the fourth day.
    The number of reports he filed the fifth day was

    A. 748   B. 165   C. 775   D. 565

18. The number 88 is 2/5 of

    A. 123   B. 141   C. 220   D. 440

19. If the product of 8.3 multiplied by .42 is subtracted from the product of 156 multiplied by .09, the result is MOST NEARLY

    A. 10.6   B. 13.7   C. 17.5   D. 20.8

20. The sum of 284.5, 3016.24, 8.9736, and 94.15 is MOST NEARLY

    A. 3402.9   B. 3403.0   C. 3403.9   D. 4036.1

21. If 8394.6 is divided by 29.17, the result is MOST NEARLY

    A. 288   B. 347   C. 2880   D. 3470

22. If two numbers are multiplied together, the result is 3752. If one of the two numbers is 56, the other number is

    A. 41   B. 15   C. 109   D. 67

23. The sum of the fractions 1/4, 2/3, 3/8, 5/6, and 3/4 is

    A. 20/33   B. 1 19/24   C. 2 1/4   D. 2 7/8

24. The fraction 7/16 expressed as a decimal is

    A. .1120   B. .2286   C. .4375   D. .4850

25. If .10 is divided by 50, the result is

    A. .002   B. .02   C. .2   D. 2

KEY (CORRECT ANSWERS)

1. B
2. A
3. D
4. B
5. D

6. A
7. A
8. C
9. B
10. D

11. B
12. D
13. C
14. B
15. C

16. D
17. C
18. C
19. A
20. C

21. A
22. D
23. D
24. C
25. A

SOLUTIONS TO PROBLEMS

1. 10,376 - 8492 = 1884

2. $155.22 - $93.75 = $61.47

3. $22.50 - $13.78 = $8.72

4. (485)(32) = 15,520

5. ($3.29)(14) = $46.06

6. (106)(318) = 33,708

7. (119)(1.15) = 136.85

8. 432 ÷ 16 = 27

9. $115.65÷5=$23.13

10. 18,711÷63=297

11. 327.45 ÷ .15 = 2183

12. 637.894 + 8352.16 + 4.8673 + 301.5 = 9296.4213 ≈ 9296.4

13. 30 ÷ .06 = 500

14. $\frac{1}{3}+\frac{4}{6}+\frac{3}{4}+\frac{1}{2}+\frac{1}{12}=\frac{4}{12}+\frac{8}{12}+\frac{9}{12}+\frac{6}{12}+\frac{1}{12}=\frac{28}{12}=2\frac{1}{3}$

15. 96,934.42 ÷ 53.496 ≈ 1811.99 ≈ 1812

16. Let x = number. Then, .25x = 48. Solving, x = 192.

17. Let x = number of reports on 5th day. Then, (610 + 720 + 740 + 755 + x)/5 = 720. Simplifying, 2825 + x = 3600, so x = 775.

18. $88÷\frac{2}{5}=220$

19. (156)(.09) - (8.3)(.42) = 10.554 ≈ 10.6

20. 284.5 + 3016.24 + 8.9736 + 94.15 = 3403.8636 ≈ 3403.9

21. $8394.6 \div 29.17 \approx 287.78 \approx 288$

22. The other number $= 3752 \div 56 = 67$

23. $\dfrac{1}{4}+\dfrac{2}{3}+\dfrac{3}{8}+\dfrac{5}{6}+\dfrac{3}{4}=\dfrac{6}{24}+\dfrac{16}{24}+\dfrac{9}{24}+\dfrac{20}{24}+\dfrac{18}{24}=\dfrac{69}{24}=2\dfrac{7}{8}$

24. $\dfrac{7}{16}=.4375$

25. $.10 \div 50 = .002$

ARITHMETICAL REASONING

EXAMINATION SECTION

TEST 1

DIRECTIONS: Each question or incomplete statement is followed by several suggested answers or completions. Select the one that BEST answers the question or completes the statement. *PRINT THE LETTER OF THE CORRECT ANSWER IN THE SPACE AT THE RIGHT.*

1. The ABC Corporation had a gross income of $125,500.00 in 2019. Of this, it paid 60% for overhead.
   If the gross income for 2020 increased by $6,500 and the cost of overhead increased to 61% of gross income, how much MORE did it pay for overhead in 2020 than in 2019?
   A. $1,320   B. $5,220   C. $7,530   D. $8,052

   1.____

2. After one year, Mr. Richards paid back a total of $16,950 as payment for a $15,000 loan. All the money paid over $15,000 was simple interest.
   The interest charge was MOST NEARLY
   A. 13%   B. 11%   C. 9%   D. 7%

   2.____

3. A checking account has a balance of $253.36.
   If deposits of $36.95, $210.23, and $7.34 and withdrawals of $117.35, $23.37, and $15.98 are made, what is the NEW balance of the account?
   A. $155.54   B. $351.18   C. $364.58   D. $664.58

   3.____

4. In 2020, the W Realty Company spent 27% of its income on rent.
   If it earned $97,254 in 2020, the amount it paid for rent was
   A. $26,258.58   B. 26,348.58   C. $27,248.58   D. $27,358.58

   4.____

5. Six percent simple annual interest on $2,436.18 is MOST NEARLY
   A. $145.08   B. $145.17   C. $146.08   D. $146.17

   5.____

6. H. Partridge receives a weekly gross salary (before deductions) of $397.50. Through weekly payroll deductions of $13.18, he is paying back a loan he took from his pension fund.
   If other fixed weekly deductions amount to $122.76, how much pay would Mr. Partridge take home over a period of 33 weeks?
   A. $7,631.28   B. $8,250.46   C. $8,631.48   D. $13,117.50

   6.____

7. Mr. Robertson is a city employee enrolled in a city retirement system. He has taken out a loan from the retirement fund and is paying it back at the rate of $14.90 every two weeks.
   In eighteen weeks, how much money will he have paid back on the loan?
   A. $268.20   B. $152.80   C. $134.10   D. $67.05

   7.____

2 (#1)

8. In 2019, The Iridor Book Company had the following expenses: rent, $6,500; overhead, $52,585; inventory, $35,700; and miscellaneous, $1,275.
If all of these expenses went up 18% in 2020, what would they TOTAL in 2020?
A. $17,290.80 B. $78,769.20 C. $96,060.00 D. $113,350.80

8.____

9. Ms. Ranier had a gross salary of $710.72 paid once every two weeks.
If the deductions from each paycheck are $125.44, $50.26, $12.58, and $2.54, how much money would Ms. Ranier take home in eight weeks?
A. $2,079.60 B. $2,842.88 C. $4,159.20 D. $5,685.76

9.____

10. Mr. Martin had a net income of $95,500 in 2019.
If he spent 34% on rent and household expenses, 3% on house furnishings, 25% on clothes, and 36% on food, how much was left for savings and other expenses?
A. $980 B. $1,910 C. $3,247 D. $9,800

10.____

11. Mr. Elsberg can pay back a loan of $1,800 from the city employees' retirement system if he pays back $36.69 every two weeks for two full years.
At the end of the two years, how much more than the original $1,800 he borrowed will Mr. Elsberg have paid back?
A. $53.94 B. $107.88 C. $190.79 D. $214.76

11.____

12. Mr. Nusbaum is a city employee receiving a gross salary (salary before deductions) of $20,800. Every two weeks, the following deductions are taken out of his salary: Federal Income Tax, $162.84; FICA, $44.26; State Tax, $29.2; City Tax, $13.94; Health Insurance, $3.14.
If Mr. Nusbaum's salary and deductions remained the same for a full calendar year, what would his net salary (gross salary less deductions) be in that year?
A. $6,596.20 B. $14,198.60 C. $18,745.50 D. $20,546.30

12.____

13. Add: 8936, 7821, 8953, 4297, 9785, 6579.
A. 45,371 B. 45,381 C. 46,371 D. 46,381

13.____

14. Multiply: 987
        867
A. 854,609 B. 854,729 C. 855,709 D. 855,729

14.____

15. Divide: 59)321439.0
A. 5438.1 B. 5447.1 C. 5448.1 D. 5457.1

15.____

16. Divide: .052)721
A. 12,648.0 B. 12,648.1 C. 12,649.0 D. 12,649.1

16.____

17. If the total number of employees in one city agency increased from 1,927 to 2,006 during a certain year, the percentage increase in the number of employees for that year is MOST NEARLY
A. 4% B. 5% C. 6% D. 7%

17.____

18. During a single fiscal year, which totaled 248 workdays, one account clerk verified 1,488 purchase vouchers.
Assuming a normal work week of five days, what is the AVERAGE number of vouchers verified by the account clerk in a one-week period during this fiscal year?
A. 25   B. 30   C. 35   D. 40

19. Multiplying a number by .75 is the same as
A. multiplying it by ²/₃
B. dividing it by ²/₃
C. multiplying it by ¾
D. dividing it by ¾

20. In City Agency A, ²/₃ of the employees are enrolled in a retirement system. City Agency B has the same number of employees as Agency A and 60% of these are enrolled in a retirement system.
If Agency A has a total of 660 employees, how many MORE employees does it have enrolled in a retirement system than does Agency B?
A. 36   B. 44   C. 56   D. 66

21. Net worth is equal to assets minus liabilities.
If, at the end of 2019, a textile company had assets of $98,695.83 and liabilities of $59,238.29, what was its net worth?
A. $38,478.54   B. $38,488.64   C. $39,457.54   D. $48,557.54

22. Mr. Martin's assets consist of the following: Cash on hand, $5,233.74, Automobile, $3,206.09; Furniture, $4,925.00; Government Bonds, $5,500.00; and House, $36,69.85.
What are his TOTAL assets?
A. $54,545.68   B. $54,455.68   C. $55,455.68   D. $55,555.68

23. If Mr. Mitchell has $627.04 in his checking account and then writes three checks for $241.75, $13.24, and $102.97, what will be his new balance?
A. $257.88   B. $269.08   C. $357.96   D. $369.96

24. An employee's net pay is equal to his total earnings less all deductions.
If an employee's total earnings in a pay period are $497.05, what is his net pay if he has the following deductions: Federal Income Tax, $18.79; City Tax, $7.25; Pension, $1.88?
A. $351.17   B. $351.07   C. $350.17   D. $350.07

25. A petty cash fund had an opening balance of $85.75 on December 1. Expenditures of $23.00, $15.65, $5.23, $14.75, and $26.38 were made out of this fund during the first 14 days of the month. Then, on December 17, another $38.50 was added to the fund.
If additional expenditures of $17.18, $3.29, and $11.64 were made during the remainder of the month, what was the FINAL balance of the petty cash fund at the end of December?
A. $6.93   B. $7.13   C. $46.51   D. $91.40

KEY (CORRECT ANSWERS)

1. B
2. A
3. B
4. A
5. D

6. C
7. C
8. D
9. A
10. B

11. B
12. B
13. C
14. D
15. C

16. D
17. A
18. B
19. C
20. B

21. C
22. D
23. B
24. D
25. B

5 (#1)

SOLUTIONS TO PROBLEMS

1. ($132,000)(.61) − ($125,500)(.60) = $5,220

2. Interest = $1,950. As a percent, $1950 ÷ 15,000 = 13%

3. New balance = $253.36 + $36.95 + $210.23 + $7.34 - $117.35 - $23.37 - $15.98 = $351.18

4. Rent = ($97,254)(.27) = $26,258.58

5. ($2,436.18)(.06) ≈ $146.17

6. ($397.50 - $13.18 - $122.76) = $8,631.48

7. ($14.90)$(\frac{18}{2})$ = $134.10

8. ($6,500 + $52,585 + $35,700 + $1,275)(1.18) = $113,350.80

9. ($710.72 - $125.44 - $50.26 - $12.58 - $2.54)$(\frac{8}{2})$ = $2,079.60

10. (1 - .34 - .03 - .25 - .36) - $1,800 = $107.88

11. (36.69)(52) - $1,800 = $107.88

12. $20,800 − (26)($162.84+$44.26+$29.72+$13.94+$3.14) = $14,198.60

13. 8,936 + 7,821 + 8,953 + 4,297 + 9,785 + 6,579 = 46,371

14. (987)(867) − 855,729

15. 321,439 ÷ 59 ≈ 5,448.1

16. 721 ÷ .057 ≈ 12,649.1

17. (2,006-1,927) ÷ 1,927 ≈ 4%

18. Let x = number of vouchers. Then, $\frac{x}{5} = \frac{1488}{248}$. Solving, x = 30

19. Multiplying by .75 is equivalent to multiplying by $\frac{3}{4}$

20. (660)$(\frac{2}{3})$ − (660)(.60) = 44

21. Net worth = $98,695.83 - $59,238.29 = $39,457.54

22. Total Assets = $5,233.74 + $3,206.09 + $4,925.00 + $5,500.00) + $36,690.85 = $55,555.68.

23. New balance = $627.04 - $241.75 - $13.24 - $102.97 = $269.08

24. Net pay = $497.05 - $90.32 - $28.74 - $18.79 - $7.25 - $1.88 = $350.07

25. Final balance = $85.75 - $23.00 - $15.65 - $5.23 - $14.75 - $26.38 + $38.50 - $17.18 - $3.29 - $11.64 = $7.13

TEST 2

DIRECTIONS: Each question or incomplete statement is followed by several suggested answers or completions. Select the one that BEST answers the question or completes the statement. *PRINT THE LETTER OF THE CORRECT ANSWER IN THE SPACE AT THE RIGHT.*

1. The formula for computing base salary is: Earnings equals base gross plus additional gross.
   If an employee's earnings during a particular period are in the amounts of $597.45, $535.92, $639.91, and $552.83, and his base gross salary is $525.50 per paycheck, what is the TOTAL of the additional gross earned by the employee during that period?
   A. $224.11   B. $224.21   C. $224.51   D. $244.11

   1.____

2. If a lump sum death benefit is paid by the retirement system in an amount equal to 3/7 of an employee's last yearly salary of $13,486.50, the amount of the death benefit paid is MOST NEARLY
   A. $5,749.29   B. $5,759.92   C. $5,779.92   D. $5,977.29

   2.____

3. Suppose that a member has paid 15 installments on a 28-installment loan. The percentage of the number of installments paid to the retirement system is
   A. 53.57%   B. 53.97%   C. 54.57%   D. 55.37%

   3.____

4. If an employee takes a 1-month vacation during a calendar year, the percentage of the year during which he works is MOST NEARLY
   A. 90.9%   B. 91.3%   C. 91.6%   D. 92.1%

   4.____

5. Suppose that an employee took a leave of absence totaling 7 months during a calendar year.
   Assuming the employee did not take any vacation time during the remainder of that year, the percentage of the year in which he worked is MOST NEARLY
   A. 41.7%   B. 43.3%   C. 46.5%   D. 47.1%

   5.____

6. A member has borrowed $4,725 from her funds in the retirement system. If $3,213 has been repaid, the percentage of the loan which is still outstanding is MOST NEARLY
   A. 16%   B. 32%   C. 48%   D. 68%

   6.____

7. If an employee worked only 24 weeks during the year because of illness, the portion of the year he was out of work was MOST NEARLY
   A. 46%   B. 48%   C. 51%   D. 54%

   7.____

8. If an employee purchased credit for a 16-week period of service which he had prior to rejoining the retirement system, the percentage of a year he purchased credit for was MOST NEARLY
   A. 27.9%   B. 28.8%   C. 30.7%   D. 33.3%

   8.____

9. If an employee contributes 2/11 of his yearly salary to his pension fund account, the percentage of his yearly salary which he contributes is MOST NEARLY
   A. 17.9%   B. 18.2%   C. 18.4%   D. 19.0%

10. In 2018, the maximum amount of income from which social security tax could be withheld (base salary) was $70,500. In 2020, the base salary was $82,500. The 2020 base salary represents a percentage increase over the 2018 base salary of APPROXIMATELY
    A. 15%   B. 16%   C. 17%   D. 18%

11. If 17.5% of an employee's salary is withheld for taxes, the one of the following which is the fraction of the salary withheld is
    A. 3/20   B. 8/35   C. 7/40   D. 4/25

12. If a person withdraws 42% of the funds from his account with the retirement system, the remaining balance represents a fraction of MOST NEARLY
    A. 7/13   B. 5/9   C. 7/12   D. 4/7

13. A property decreases in value from $45,000 to $35,000. The percent of decrease is MOST NEARLY
    A. 20.5%   B. 22.2%   C. 25.0%   D. 28.6%

14. The fraction $\frac{487}{101326}$ expressed as a decimal is MOST NEARLY
    A. .0482   B. .00481   C. .0049   D. .00392

15. The reciprocal of the sum of 2/3 and 1/6 can be expressed as
    A. 0.83   B. 1.20   C. 1.25   D. 1.50

16. Total land and building costs for a new commercial property equal $50 per square foot.
    If the investors expect a 10 percent return on their costs, and if total operating expenses average 5 percent of total costs, annual gross rentals per square foot must be AT LEAST
    A. $7.50   B. $8.50   C. $10.00   D. $12.00

17. The formula for computing the amount of annual deposit in a compound interest bearing account to provide a lump sum at the end of a period of years is
    $X = \frac{r \cdot L}{(1+r)^{n-1}}$ (X is the amount of annual deposit, r is the rate of interest, and n is the number of years and L = lump sum).
    Using the formula, the annual amount of the deposit at the end of each year to accumulate $20,000 at the end of 3 years with interest at 2 percent on annual balances is
    A. $6,120.00   B. $6,203.33   C. $6,535.09   D. $6,666.66

3 (#2)

18. An investor sold two properties at $150,000 each. On one he made a 2.5 percent profit. On the other, he suffered a 25 percent loss.
The NET result of his sales was
   A. neither a gain nor a loss
   B. a $20,000 loss
   C. a $75,000 gain
   D. a $75,000 loss

18.____

19. A contractor decides to install a chain fence covering the perimeter of a parcel 75 feet wide and 112 feet in depth.
Which one of the following represents the number of feet to be covered?
   A. 187   B. 364   C. 374   D. 8,400

19.____

20. A builder estimates he can build an average of 4½ one-family homes to an acre. There are 640 acres to one square mile.
Which one of the following CORRECTLY represents the number of one-family homes the builder would estimate he can build on one square mile?
   A. 1,280   B. 1,920   C. 2,560   D. 2,880

20.____

21. $.01059 deposit at 7 percent interest will yield $1.00 in 30 years.
If a person deposited $1,059 at 7 percent interest on April 4, 1991, which one of the following amounts would represent the worth of this deposit on March 31, 2021?
   A. $100   B. $1,000   C. $10,000   D. $100,000

21.____

22. A building has an economic life of forty years.
Assuming the building depreciates at a constant annual rate, which one of the following CORRECTLY represents the yearly percentage of depreciation?
   A. 2.0%   B. 2.5%   C. 5.0%   D. 7.0%

22.____

23. A building produces a gross income of $200,000 with a net income of $20,000, before mortgage charges and capital recapture. The owner is able to increase the gross income 5 percent without a corresponding increase in operating costs.
The effect upon the net income will be an INCREASE of
   A. 5%   B. 10%   C. 12.5%   D. 50%

23.____

24. The present value of $1.00 not payable for 8 years, and at 10 percent interest, is $.4665.
Which of the following amounts represents the PRESENT value of $1,000 payable 8 years hence at 10 percent interest?
   A. $46.65   B. $466.50   C. $4,665.00   D. $46,650.00

24.____

25. The amount of real property taxes to be levied by a city is $100 million. The assessment roll subject to taxation shows an assessed valuation of $2 billion.
Which one of the following tax rates CORRECTLY represents the tax rate to be levied per $100 of assessed valuation?
   A. $.50   B. $5.00   C. $50.00   D. $500.00

25.____

KEY (CORRECT ANSWERS)

1.	A		11.	C
2.	C		12.	C
3.	A		13.	B
4.	C		14.	B
5.	A		15.	B
6.	B		16.	A
7.	D		17.	C
8.	C		18.	B
9.	B		19.	C
10.	C		20.	D

21. D
22. B
23. D
24. B
25. B

5 (#2)

SOLUTIONS TO PROBLEMS

1. $597.45 + $535.91 + $639.91 + $552.83 = $2,326.11. Then, $2,326.11 − (4)($525.50) = $224.11

2. Death benefit = ($13,486.50)$(\frac{3}{7})$ ≈ $5,779.92

3. $\frac{15}{28}$ ≈ 53.57%

4. $\frac{11}{12}$ ≈ 91.6% (closer to 91.7%)

5. $\frac{5}{12}$ ≈ 41.7%

6. ($4,725-$3,213) ÷ $4,725 = 32%

7. $\frac{28}{52}$ ≈ 54%

8. $\frac{16}{52}$ ≈ 30.7% (closer to 30.8%)

9. $\frac{2}{11}$ ≈ 18.2%

10. ($82,500 - $70,500) ÷ $70,500 = 17%

11. 17.5% = $\frac{175}{1000}$ = $\frac{7}{40}$

12. 100% - 42% = 58% = $\frac{58}{100}$ = $\frac{29}{50}$, closest to $\frac{7}{12}$ in selections

13. $\frac{\$10,000}{\$45,000}$ ≈ 22.2%

14. 487/101,216 ≈ .00481

15. $\frac{2}{3} + \frac{1}{6} = \frac{5}{6}$ Then, $1 \div \frac{5}{6} = \frac{6}{5}$ = 1.20

16. (.15)($50) = $7.50

17. x = (.02)($20,000)/[(1+.02)^3 − 1] = 400 ÷ .061208 ≈ $6,535.09

18. Sold 150,000, 25% loss = paid 200,000, loss of $50,000 Sold 150,000, 25% profit = paid 120,000, profit of 30,000 − 50,000 + 30,000 = 20,000 (loss)

19. Perimeter = (2)(75) + (2)(112) = 374 ft.

20. (640)(4½) = 2,880 homes

21. (1÷.01059)(1059) = $100,000

22. 1÷4 = .025 = 2.5%

23. New gross income = ($200,000)(X1.05) = $210,000
    Then, ($210,000-$200,000) ÷ $20,000 = 50%

24. Let x = present value of $1,000. Then, $\frac{\$1.00}{\$.4665} = \frac{\$1000}{x}$
    Solving, x = $466.50

25. Let x = tax rate. Then, $\frac{\$100,000,000}{\$2,000,000,000} = \frac{x}{\$100}$
    Solving, x = $5.00

TEST 3

DIRECTIONS: Each question or incomplete statement is followed by several suggested answers or completions. Select the one that BEST answers the question or completes the statement. *PRINT THE LETTER OF THE CORRECT ANSWER IN THE SPACE AT THE RIGHT.*

1. It is found that for the past three years the average weekly number of inspections per inspector ranged from 20 inspections to 40 inspections.
   On the basis of this information, it is MOST reasonable to conclude that
   A. on the average, 30 inspections per week were made
   B. the average weekly number of inspections never fell below 20
   C. the performance of inspectors deteriorated over the three-year period
   D. the range in average weekly inspections was 60

   1.____

Questions 2-4.

DIRECTIONS: Questions 2 through 4 are to be answered on the basis of the following information.

The number of students admitted to University X in 2019 from High School Y was 268 students. This represented 13.7 percent of University X's entering freshman classes. In 2020, it is expected that University X will admit 591 students from High School Y, which is expected to represent 19.4 percent of the 2020 entering freshman classes of University X.

2. Which of the following is CLOSEST estimate of the size of University's expected 2020 entering freshman classes?
   _____ students
   A. 2,000   B. 2,500   C. 3,000   D. 3,500

   2.____

3. Of the following, the expected percentage of increase from 2019 to 2020 in the number of students graduating from High School Y and entering University X as freshmen is MOST NEARLY
   A. 5.7%   B. 20%   C. 45%   D. 120%

   3.____

4. Assume that the cost of processing admission to University X from High School Y in 2019 was an average of $28. Also, that this was 1/3 more than the average cost of processing each of the other 2019 freshmen admissions to University X.
   Then, the one of the following that MOST closely shows the total processing cost of all 2019 freshman admissions to University X is
   A. $6,500   B. $20,000   C. $30,000   D. $40,000

   4.____

5. Assume that during the fiscal year 2019-2020, a bureau produced 20% more work units than it produced in the fiscal year 2018-2019. Also assume that during the fiscal year 2019-2020 that bureau's staff was 20% smaller than it was in the fiscal year 2018-2019.

   5.____

125

2 (#3)

On the basis of this information, it would be MOST proper to conclude that the number of work units produced per staff member in that bureau in the fiscal year 2019-2020 exceeded the number of work units produced per staff member in that bureau in the fiscal year 2018-2019 by which one of the following percentages?
A. 20%   B. 25%   C. 40%   D. 50%

6. Assume that during the following fiscal years (FY), a bureau has received the following appropriations: 6._____
   FY 2015-2016 - $200,000
   FY 2016-2017 - $240,000
   FY 2017-2018 - $280,000
   FY 2018-2019 - $390,000
   FY 2019-2020 - $505,000

The bureau's appropriation for which one of the following fiscal years showed the LARGEST percentage of increase over the bureau's appropriation for the immediately previous fiscal year?
A. FY 2016-2017   B. FY 2017-2018
C. FY 2018-2019   D. FY 2010-2020

7. Assume that the number of buses (U_t) required for a given line-haul system serving the Central Business District depends upon roundtrip time (t), capacity of bus (c), and the total number of people to be moved in a peak hour (P) in the major direction, i.e., in the morning and out in the evening. 7._____
The formula for the number of buses required is $U_t =$
A. Ptc   B. $\frac{tP}{c}$ C. $\frac{cP}{t}$ D. $\frac{ct}{P}$

8. The area, in blocks, that can be served by a single stop for any maximum walking distance is given by the following formula: $a = 2w^2$. In this formula, a = the area served by a stop and w = maximum walking distance. 8._____
If people will tolerate a walk of up to three blocks, how many stops would be needed to service an area of 288 square blocks?
A. 9   B. 16   C. 18   D. 27

Questions 9-11.

DIRECTIONS: Questions 9 through 11 are to be answered on the basis of the following information.

In 2019, a police precinct records 456 cases of car thefts, which is 22.6 percent of all grand larcenies. In 2020, there were 560 such cases, which constituted 35% of the broader category.

9. The number of crimes in the broader category in 2020 was MOST NEARLY 9._____
A. 1,600   B. 1,700   C. 1,960   D. 2,800

10. The change from 2019 to 2020 in the number of crimes in the broader category represented MOST NEARLY a
    A. 2.5% decrease
    B. 10.1% increase
    C. 12.5% increase
    D. 20% decrease

    10.____

11. In 2020, one out of every 6 of these crimes was solved. This represents MOST NEARLY what percentage of the total number of crimes in the broader category that year?
    A. 5.8
    B. 6
    C. 9.3
    D. 12

    11.____

12. Assume that a maintenance shop does 5 brake jobs to every 3 front-end jobs. It does 8,000 jobs altogether in a 240-day year. In one day, one worker can do 3 front-end jobs or 4 brake jobs.
    About how many workers will be needed in the shop?
    A. 3
    B. 5
    C. 10
    D. 18

    12.____

13. Assume that the price of a certain item declines by 6% one year, and then increases by 5 and 10 percent, respectively, during the next two years.
    What is the OVERALL increase in price over the three-year period?
    A. 4.2
    B. 6
    C. 8.6
    D. 10.1

    13.____

14. After finding the total percent change in a price (TO) over a three-year period, as in the preceding question, one could compute the average annual percent change in the price by using the formula
    A. $(1+TC)^{1/3}$
    B. $\frac{(1+TC)}{3}$
    C. $(1+TC)^{1/3-1}$
    D. $\frac{1}{(1+TC)^{1/3}-1}$

    14.____

15. 357 is 6% of
    A. 2,142
    B. 5,950
    C. 4,140
    D. 5,900

    15.____

16. In 2019, a department bought n pieces of a certain supply item for a total of $x. In 2020, the department bought k percent fewer of the item but had to pay a total of g percent more for it.
    Which of the following formulas is CORRECT for determining the average price per item in 2020?
    A. $100\frac{xg}{nk}$
    B. $\frac{x(100+g)}{n(100-k)}$
    C. $\frac{x(100-g)}{n(100+k)}$
    D. $\frac{x}{n} - 100\frac{g}{k}$

    16.____

17. A sample of 18 income tax returns, each with 4 personal exemptions, is taken for 2019 and 2020. The breakdown is as follows in terms of income:

Average Gross Income (in thousands)	Number of Returns	
	2019	2020
40	6	2
80	10	11
120	2	5

    There is a personal deduction per exemption of $500.
    There are no other expense deductions. In addition, there is an exclusion of $3,000 for incomes less than $50,000 and $2,000 for incomes from $50,000 to $99,999.99. From $100,000 upward there is no exclusion.

    17.____

The average net taxable income for the samples in thousands for 2019 is MOST NEARLY
A. $67   B. $85   C. $10   D. $128

18. In the preceding question, the increase in average net taxable income for the sample (in thousands) between 2019 and 2020 is
A. 16   B. 20   C. 24   D. 34

19. Assume that supervisor S has four subordinates—A, B, C, and D. The MAXIMUM number of relationships, assuming that all combinations are included, that can exist between S and his subordinates is
A. 28   B. 15   C. 7   D. 4

20. If the workmen's compensation insurance rate for clerical workers is 93 cents per $100 of wages, the total premium paid by a city whose clerical staff earns $8,765,000 is MOST NEARLY
A. $8,150   B. $81,515   C. $87,650   D. $93,765

21. Assume that a budget of $3,240,000,000 for the fiscal year beginning July 1, 2020 has been approved. A city sales tax is expected to provide $1,100,000,000; licenses, fees and sundry revenues ae expected to yield $121,600,000; the balance is to be raised from property taxes. A tax equalization board has appraised all property in the city at a fair value of $42,500,000,000. The council wishes to assess property at 60% of its fair value.
The tax rate would need to be MOST NEARLY _____ per $100 of assessed value.
A. $12.70   B. $10.65   C. $7.90   D. $4.00

22. Men's white linen handkerchiefs cost $12.90 for 3. The cost per dozen handkerchiefs is
A. $77.40   B. $38.70   C. $144.80   D. $51.60

23. Assume that it is necessary to partition a room measuring 40 feet by 20 feet into eight smaller rooms of equal size.
Allowing no room for aisles, the MINIMUM amount of partitioning that would be needed is _____ feet.
A. 90   B. 100   C. 110   D. 140

24. Assume that two types of files have been ordered: 200 of type A and 100 of type B. When the files are delivered, the buyer discovers that 25% of each type is damaged. Of the remaining files, 20% of type A and 40% of type B are the wrong color.
The total number of files that are the WRONG COLOR is
A. 30   B. 40   C. 50   D. 60

5 (#3)

25. In a unit of five inspectors, one inspector makes an average of 12 inspections a day, two inspectors make an average of 10 inspections a day, and two inspectors make an average of 9 inspections a day.
If in a certain week one of the inspectors who makes an average of nine inspections a day is out of work on Monday and Tuesday because of illness and all the inspectors do no inspections for half a day on Wednesday because of a special meeting, the number of inspections this unit can be expected to make in that week is MOST NEARLY
   A. 215   B. 225   C. 230   D. 250

25.____

KEY (CORRECT ANSWERS)

1. B
2. C
3. D
4. D
5. D

6. C
7. B
8. B
9. A
10. D

11. A
12. C
13. C
14. C
15. B

16. B
17. A
18. A
19. B
20. B

21. C
22. D
23. B
24. D
25. A

SOLUTIONS TO PROBLEMS

1. Since the number of weekly inspections ranged from 20 to 40, this implies that the average weekly number of inspections never fell below 20.

2. 591 ÷ 194 ≈ 3046, closest to 3,000 students

3. (591-268) ÷ 268 = 120%

4. Total processing cost = (268)(28) + (1,688)($21) = $42,952, closest to $40,000. [Note: Since 268 represents 13.7%, total freshman population = 268 ÷ .137 ≈ 1,956. Then, 1,956 − 268 = 1,688]

5. Let x = staff size in 2018-2019. Then, .80x = staff size in 2019-2020. Since the 2019-2020 staff produced 20% more work, this is represented by 1.20. However, to measure the productivity per staff member, the factor 1/.80 = 1.25 must also be used to equate the 2 staffs. Then, (1.20)(1.25) = 1.50. Thus, the 2019-2020 staff produced 50% more than the 2018-2019 staff.

6. The respective percent increases are ≈ 20%, 17%, 39%, 29%. The largest would be, over the previous fiscal year, for the current fiscal year 2018-2019

7. $\frac{P}{c}$ = number of buses needed per hour. If t = time (in hrs.), then U_t = tP.c

8. a = (2)(9) = 18 for 1 stop. Then, 288 ÷ 18 = 15 stops.

9. 560 ÷ .35 = 1600 grand larcenies.

10. 456 ÷ .226 = 2018; 560 ÷ .35 = 1600. Then, (1,600-2,018) ÷ 2,018 = -20% or a 20% decrease.

11. $(\frac{1}{6})(560) = 93\frac{1}{3}$. Then, $93\frac{1}{3}$ ÷ 1,600 = 5.8%

12. There are 5,000 brake jobs and 3,000 front-end jobs in one year.
    5,000 ÷ 4 = 1,250 days, and 1,250 ÷ 240 ≈ 5.2. Also, 3,000 ÷ 3 = 1,000 days, and 1,000 ÷ 240 ≈ 4.2. Total number of workers needed ≈ 5.2 + 4.2 ≈ 10.

13. (.94)(1.05)(1.10) = 1.0857, which represents an overall increase by about 8.6%.

14. Average annual % change = $(1+TC)^{1/3} - 1 = (1.0857)^{1/3} - 1 ≈ 2.8\%$.

15. 357 ÷ .06 = 5,950

16. In 2020, $(h)(1-\frac{k}{100})$ pieces cost $(x)(1 + \frac{g}{100})$ dollars. To calculate the cost for 1 piece (average cost), find the value of $[(x)(1 + \frac{G}{100})] ÷ [(n)(1 - \frac{K}{100})] = [(x)(100+g)/100]$. [100/{n(100-k)}] = [x(100+g)]/[n(100-k)]

7 (#3)

17.

	#	Deductions Up to 50,000	
40,000	6	2000	3000
80,000	10	2000	2000
20,000	2	2000	

40,000−3,000−2,000 = 35,000 × 6
80,000−2,000−2,000 = 76,000 × 10
= 118000 × 2

35,000 × 6 = 210,000 = 210
76,000 × 10 = 760,000 = 760
118,800 × 2 = 236,000 = 236
              1206

1206 ÷ 18 = 67

18. 2020

	#	Deductions	
40,000	2	2000	3000
80,000	11	2000	2000
120,000	5	2000	

35,000 × 2 =   70,000
76,000 × 11 = 836,000
118,000 × 5 = 590,000
              1,496,000

1,496,000/18 = 83,111
83,111 − 67,000 = 16,111 = most nearly 16 (in thousands)

19. We are actually looking for the number of different groups of different sizes involving S. This reduces to $_4C_1 + {_4C_2} + {_4C_2} + {_4C_4} = 4 + 6 + 4 + 1 = 15$. The notation $_nC_r$ means combinations of n things taken R at a time = $[(n)(n-1)(n-2)(\ldots)(n-R+1)]/[(R)(R-1)(\ldots)(1)]$. The 15 groups are: SA, SB, SC, SD, SAB, SAC, SAD, SBC, SBD, SCD, SABC, SABD, SACD, SBCD, SABCD.

20. Let x = total premiums. Then, $\frac{.93}{100} = \frac{X}{8,765,000}$ Solving, x = $81,515

21. The balance, raised from property taxes, = $3,240,000,000 − $1,100,000,000 − $121,600,000 = $2,018,400,000. Now, (.60)($42,500,000,000) = $25,500,000. The tax rate per $100 of assessed value = ($2,018,400,000)($100)(/$25,500,000,00 = $7.90.

22. A dozen costs ($12.90)($\frac{12}{3}$) = $51.60.

23. (40(20) ÷ 8 = 100 ft.

24. Total number of wrong-color files = (200)(.75)(.20)+(100)(.75)(.40) = 60

25. Weekly number of inspections = (12×5) + (10×5) + (10×5) + (9×5) + 9×5) = 250
Subtract: 9 Monday, 9 Tuesday, 25 Wednesday
Total: 250 − 9 − 9 − 25 = 207
Closest entry is choice A.

READING COMPREHENSION
UNDERSTANDING AND INTERPRETING
WRITTEN MATERIAL

COMMENTARY

The ability to read and understand written materials—texts, publications, newspapers, orders, directions, expositions—is a skill basic to a functioning democracy and to an efficient business or viable government.

That is why almost all examinations—for beginning, middle, and senior levels—test reading comprehension, directly or indirectly.

The reading test measures how well you understand what you read. This is how it is done: You read a short paragraph and five statements. From the five statements, you choose the one statement, or answer, that is BEST supported by, or best matches, what is said in the paragraph.

SAMPLE QUESTIONS

DIRECTIONS: Each question has five suggested answers, lettered A, B, C, D, and E. Decide which one is the BEST answer. *PRINT THE LETTER OF THE CORRECT ANSWER IN THE SPACE AT THE RIGHT.*

1. The prevention of accidents makes it necessary not only that safety devices be used to guard exposed machinery but also that mechanics be instructed in safety rules which they must follow for their own protection and that the light in the plant be adequate.
   The paragraph BEST supports the statement that industrial accidents
   A. are always avoidable
   B. may be due to ignorance
   C. usually result from inadequate machinery
   D. cannot be entirely overcome
   E. result in damage to machinery

1.____

2

ANALYSIS

Remember what you have to do:
- First - Read the paragraph
- Second - Decide what the paragraph means
- Third - Read the five suggested answers.
- Fourth - Select the one answer which BEST matches what the paragraph says or is BEST supported by something in the paragraph. (Sometimes you may have to read the paragraph again in order to be sure which suggested answer is best.)

This paragraph is talking about three steps that should be taken to prevent industrial accidents
1. Use safety devices on machines
2. Instruct mechanics in safety rules
3. provide adequate lighting

SELECTION

With this in mind, let's look at each suggested answer. Each one starts with "Industrial accidents…"

SUGGESTED ANSWER A
Industrial accidents (A) are always avoidable.
(The paragraph talks about how to avoid accidents, but does not say that accidents are always avoidable.)

SUGGESTED ANSWER B
Industrial accidents (B) may be due to ignorance.
(One of the steps given in the paragraph to prevent accidents is to instruct mechanics on safety rules. This suggests that lack of knowledge or ignorance of safety rules causes accidents. This suggested answer sounds like a good possibility for being the right answer.)

SUGGESTED ANSWER C
Industrial accidents (C) usually result from inadequate machinery.
(The paragraph does suggest that exposed machines cause accidents, but it doesn't say that it is the usual cause of accidents. The word usually makes this a wrong answer.)

SUGGESTED ANSWER D
Industrial accidents (D) cannot be entirely overcome.
(You may know from your own experience that this is a true statement. But that is not what the paragraph is talking about. Therefore, it is NOT the correct answer.)

SUGGESTED ANSWER E
Industrial accidents (E) result in damage to machinery.
(This is a statement that may or may not be true, but in any case it is NOT covered by the paragraph.)

Looking back, you see that the one suggested answer of the five given that BEST matches what the paragraph says is: Industrial accidents (B) may be due to ignorance.

The CORRECT answer then is B.

Be sure to read ALL the possible answers before you make your choice. You may think that none of the five answers is really good, but choose the BEST one of the five.

---

2. Probably few people realize, as they drive on a concrete road, that steel is used to keep the surface flat in spite of the weight of the busses and trucks. Steel bars, deeply embedded in the concrete, provide sinews to take the stresses so that the stresses cannot crack the slab or make it wavy.
The paragraph BEST supports the statement that a concrete road
    A. is expensive to build
    B. usually cracks under heavy weights
    C. looks like any other road
    D. is used only for heavy traffic
    E. is reinforced with other material

2.____

ANALYSIS

This paragraph is commenting on the fact that
1. few people realize, as they drive on a concrete road, that steel is deeply embedded
2. steel keeps the surface flat
3. steel bars enable the road to take the stresses without cracking or becoming wavy

SELECTION

Now read and think about the possible answers:
    A. A concrete road is expensive to build. (Maybe so but that is not what the paragraph is about.)
    B. A concrete road usually cracks under heavy weights. (The paragraph talks about using steel bars to prevent heavy weights from cracking concrete roads. It says nothing about how usual it is for the roads to crack. The word usually makes this suggested answer wrong.)
    C. A concrete road looks like any other road. (This may or may not be true. The important thing to note is that it has nothing to do with what the paragraph is about.)
    D. A concrete road is used only for heavy traffic. (This answer at least has something to do with the paragraph—concrete roads are used with heavy traffic—but it does not say "used only.")
    E. A concrete road is reinforced with other material. (This choice seems to be the correct one on two counts: First, the paragraph does suggest that concrete roads are made

stronger by embedding steel bars in them. This is another way of saying "concrete roads are reinforced with steel bars." Second, by the process of elimination, the other four choices are ruled out as correct answers simply because they do not apply.)

You can be sure that not all the reading questions will be so easy as these.

HINTS FOR ANSWERING READING QUESTIONS

1. Read the paragraph carefully. Then read each suggested answer carefully. Read every word, because often one word can make the difference between a right and a wrong answer.

2. Choose that answer which is supported in the paragraph itself. Do not choose an answer which is a correct statement unless it is based on information in the paragraph.

3. Even though a suggested answer has many of the words used in the paragraph, it may still be wrong.

4. Look out for words—such as *always*, *never*, *entirely*, or *only*—which tend to make a suggested answer wrong.

5. Answer first those questions which you can answer most easily. Then work on the other questions.

6. If you can't figure out the answer to the question, guess.

READING COMPREHENSION
UNDERSTANDING AND INTERPRETING WRITTEN MATERIAL
EXAMINATION SECTION
TEST 1

DIRECTIONS: All questions are to be answered SOLELY on the basis of the information contained in the passage. Each question or incomplete statement is followed by several suggested answers or completions. Select the one that BEST answers the question or completes the statement. *PRINT THE LETTER OF THE CORRECT ANSWER IN THE SPACE AT THE RIGHT.*

Questions 1-7.

Snow-covered roads spell trouble for motorists all winter long. Clearing highways of snow and ice to keep millions of motor vehicles moving freely is a tremendous task. Highway departments now rely, to a great extent, on chemical de-icers to get the big job done. Sodium chloride, in the form of commercial salt, is the de-icer most frequently used.

There is no reliable evidence to prove that salt reduces highway accidents. But available statistics are impressive. For example, before Massachusetts used chemical de-icers, it had a yearly average of 21 fatal accidents and 1,635 injuries attributed to cars skidding on snow or ice. Beginning in 1990, the state began fighting hazardous driving conditions with chemical de-icers. During the period 1990-2000, there was a yearly average of only seven deaths and 736 injuries as a result of skids.

Economical and effective in a moderately low temperature range, salt is increasingly popular with highway departments, but not so popular with individual car owners. Salty slush eats away at metal, including auto bodies. It also sprinkles windshields with a fine-grained spray which dries on contact, severely reducing visibility. However, drivers who are hindered or immobilized by heavy winter weather favor the liberal use of products such as sodium chloride. When snow blankets roads, these drivers feel that the quickest way to get back to the safety of driving on bare pavement is through use of de-icing salts.

1. The MAIN reason given by the above passage for the use of sodium chloride as a de-icer is that it
   A. has no harmful effects
   B. is economical
   C. is popular among car owners
   D. reduces highway accidents

1.____

2. The above passage may BEST be described as a(n)
   A. argument against the use of sodium chloride as a de-icer
   B. discussion of some advantages and disadvantages of sodium chloride as a de-icer
   C. recommendation to use sodium chloride as a de-icer
   D. technical account of the uses and effects of sodium chloride as a de-icer

2.____

3. Based on the above passage, the use of salt on snow-covered roadways will eventually
   A. decrease the efficiency of the automobile fuel
   B. cause tires to deteriorate
   C. damage the surface of the roadway
   D. cause holes in the sides of cars

4. The average number of persons killed yearly in Massachusetts in car accidents caused by skidding on snow or ice, before chemical de-icers were used there, was
   A. 9   B. 12   C. 21   D. 30

5. According to the above passage, it would be advisable to use salt as a de-icer when
   A. outdoor temperatures are somewhat below freezing
   B. residues on highway surfaces are deemed to be undesirable
   C. snow and ice have low absorbency characteristics
   D. the use of a substance is desired which dries on contact

6. As a result of using chemical de-icers, the number of injuries resulting from skids in Massachusetts was reduced by about
   A. 35%   B. 45%   C. 55%   D. 65%

7. According to the above passage, driver visibility can be severely reduced by
   A. sodium chloride deposits on the windshield
   B. glare from salt and snow crystals
   C. salt spray covering the front lights
   D. faulty windshield wipers

Questions 8-10.

An employee should call the Fire Department for any fire except a small one in a wastebasket. This kind of fire can be put out with a fire extinguisher. If the employee is not sure about the size of the fire, he should not wait to find out how big it is. He should call the Fire Department at once.

Every employee should know what to do when a fire starts. He should know how to use the firefighting tools in the building and how to call the Fire Department. He should also know where the nearest fire alarm box is. But the most important thing for an employee to do in case of fire is to avoid panic.

8. If there is a small fire in a wastebasket, an employee should
   A. call the Fire Department   B. let it burn itself out
   C. open a window   D. put it out with a fire extinguisher

9. In case of fire, the MOST important thing for an employee to do is to
   A. find out how big it is   B. keep calm
   C. leave the building right away D. report to his boss

10. If a large fire starts while he is at work, an employee should always FIRST
    A. call the Fire Department
    B. notify the Housing Superintendent
    C. remove inflammables from the building
    D. use a fire extinguisher

Questions 11-12.

Those correction theorists who are in agreement with severe and rigid controls as a normal part of the correctional process are confronted with a contradiction; this is so because a responsibility which is consistent with freedom cannot be developed in a repressive atmosphere. They do not recognize this contradiction when they carry out their programs with dictatorial force and expect convicted criminals exposed to such programs to be reformed into free and responsible citizens.

11. According to the above passage, those correction theorists are faced with a contradiction who
    A. are in favor of the enforcement of strict controls in a prison
    B. believe that to develop a sense of responsibility, freedom must not be restricted
    C. take the position that the development of responsibility consistent with freedom is not possible in a repressive atmosphere
    D. think that freedom and responsibility can be developed only in a democratic atmosphere

12. According to the above passage, a repressive atmosphere in a prison
    A. does not conform to present-day ideas of freedom of the individual
    B. is admitted by correction theorists to be in conflict with the basic principles of the normal correctional process
    C. is advocated as the best method of maintaining discipline when rehabilitation is of secondary importance
    D. is not suitable for the development of a sense of responsibility consistent with freedom

Questions 13-16.

Abandoned cars—with tires gone, chrome stripped away, and windows smashed—have become a common sight on the City's streets. In 2020, more than 72,000 were deposited at curbs by owners who never came back, an increase of 15,000 from the year before and more than 30 times the number abandoned a decade ago. In January, 2021, the City's Environmental Protection Administrator asked the State Legislature to pass a law requiring a buyer of a new automobile to deposit $100 and an owner of an automobile at the time the law takes effect to deposit $50 with the State Department of Motor Vehicles. In return, they would be given a certificate of deposit which would be passed on to each succeeding owner. The final owner would get the deposit money back if he could present proof that he has disposed of his car "in an environmentally acceptable manner." The Legislature has given no indication that it plans to rush ahead on the matter.

13. The number of cars abandoned in City streets in 2010 was MOST NEARLY 13.____
    A. 2,500   B. 12,000   C. 27,500   D. 57,000

14. The proposed law would require a person who owned a car bought before the 14.____
    law was passed to deposit
    A. $100 with the State Department of Motor Vehicles
    B. $50 with the Environmental Protection Administration
    C. $100 with the State Legislature
    D. $50 with the State Department of Motor Vehicles

15. The proposed law would require the State to return the deposit money only 15.____
    when the
    A. original owner of the car shows roof that he sold it
    B. last owner of the car shows proof that he got rid of the car in a
       satisfactory way
    C. owner of the car shows proof that he has transferred the certificate of
       deposit to the next owner
    D. last owner of a car returns the certificate of deposit

16. The MAIN idea or theme of the above article is that 16.____
    A. a proposed new law would make it necessary for car owners in the State
       to pay additional taxes
    B. the State Legislature is against a proposed law to require deposits from
       automobile owners to prevent them from abandoning their cars
    C. the City is trying to find a solution for the increasing number of cars
       abandoned on its streets
    D. to pay for the removal of abandoned cars, the City's Environmental
       Protection Administrator has asked the State to fine automobile owners
       who abandon their vehicles

Questions 17-19.

The German roach is the most common roach in houses in the United State. Adults are pale brown and about ½-inch long; both sexes have wings as long as the body, and can be distinguished from other roaches by the two dark stripes on the pronotum. The female carries its egg capsule protruding from her abdomen until the eggs are ready to hatch. This is the only common house-infesting species which carries the egg capsule for such an extended period of time. A female will usually produce 4 to 8 capsules in her lifetime. Each capsule contains 30 to 48 eggs which hatch out in about 28 days at ordinary room temperature. The completion of the nymph stage under room conditions requires 40 to 125 days. German roaches may live as adults for as long as 303 days.

It is stated about that the German cockroach is the most commonly encountered of the house-infesting species in the United States. The reasons for this are somewhat complex, but the understanding of some of the factors involved are basic to the practice of pest control. In the first place, the German cockroach has a larger number of eggs per capsule and a shorter hatching time than do the other species. It also requires a shorter period from hatching until sexual maturity, so that within a given period of time a population of German roaches will produce a larger number of eggs. Onn the basis of this fact, we can state that this species has a high reproductive potential. Since the female carries the egg capsule during nearly the entire time that the embryos are developing within the egg, many hazards of the environment which may affect the eggs are avoided. This means that more nymphs are likely to hatch and that a larger portion of the reproductive potential is realized. The nymphs which hatch from each egg capsule tend to stay close to each other, and since they are often close to the female at time of hatching, there is a tendency for the population density to be high locally. Being smaller than most of the other roaches, they are able to conceal themselves in many places which are inaccessible to individuals of the larger species. All of these factors combined help to give the German cockroach an advantage with regard to group survival.

17. According to the above passage, the MOST important feature of the German roach which gives it an advantage over other roaches is
    A. distinctive markings
    B. immunity to disease
    C. long life span
    D. power to reproduce

18. An IMPORTANT difference between an adult female German roach and an adult female of other species is the
    A. black bars or stripes which appear on the abdomen of the German roach
    B. German roach's preference for warm, moist places in which to breed
    C. long period of time during which the German roach carries the egg capsule
    D. presence of longer wings on the female German roach

19. A storeroom in a certain housing project has an infestation of German roaches, which includes 125 adult female.
    If the infestation is not treated and ordinary room temperature is maintained in the storeroom, how many eggs will hatch out during the lifetime of these females if they each lay 8 capsules containing 48 eggs each?
    A. 1,500   B. 48,000   C. 96,000   D. 303,000

Questions 20-22.

City governments have long had building codes which set minimum standards for building and for human occupancy. The code (or series of codes) makes provisions for standards of lighting and ventilation, sanitation, fire prevention, and protection. As a result of demands from manufacturers, builders, real estate people, tenement owners, and building-trades unions, these codes often have established minimum standards well below those that the contemporary society would accept as a rock-bottom minimum. Codes often become outdated, so that meager standards in one era become seriously inadequate a few decades later as society's concept of a minimum standard of living changes. Out-of-date codes, when still in use, have sometimes prevented the introduction of new devices and modern building techniques. Thus, it is extremely important that building codes keep pace with changes in the accepted concept of a minimum standard of living.

20. According to the above passage, all of the following considerations in building planning would probably be covered in a building code EXCEPT
    A. closet space as a percentage of total floor area
    B. size and number of windows required for rooms of differing sizes

C. placement of fire escapes in each line of apartments
D. type of garbage disposal units to be installed

21. According to the above passage, if an ideal building code were to be created, how would the established minimum standards in it compare to the ones that are presently set by city governments?
They would
   A. be lower than they are at present
   B. be higher than they are at present
   C. be comparable to the present minimum standards
   D. vary according to the economic group that sets them

21.____

22. On the basis of the above passage, what is the reason for difficulties in introducing new building techniques?
   A. Builders prefer techniques which represent the rock-bottom minimum desired by society.
   B. Certain manufacturers have obtained patents on various building methods to the exclusion of new techniques.
   C. The government does not want to invest money in techniques that will soon be outdated.
   D. New techniques are not provided for in building codes which are not up-to-date.

22.____

Questions 23-25.

A flameproof fabric is defined as one which, when exposed to small sources of ignition such as sparks or smoldering cigarettes, does not burn beyond the vicinity of the source of the ignition. Cotton fabrics are the materials commonly used that are considered most hazardous. Other materials, such as acetate rayons and linens, are somewhat less hazardous, and woolens and some natural silk fabrics, even when untreated, are about the equal of the average treated cotton fabric insofar as flame spread and ease of ignition are concerned. The method of application is to immerse the fabric in a flameproofing solution. The container used must be large enough so that all the fabric is thoroughly wet and there are no folds which the solution does not penetrate.

23. According to the above passage, a flameproof fabric is one which
   A. is unaffected by heat and smoke
   B. resists the spread of flames when ignited
   C. burns with a cold flame
   D. cannot be ignited by sparks or cigarettes
   E. may smolder but cannot burn

23.____

24. According to the above passage, woolen fabrics which have not been flameproofed are as likely to catch fire as _____ fabrics.
   A. treated silk   B. treated acetate rayon
   C. untreated linen   D. untreated synthetic
   E. treated cotton

24.____

25. In the method described above, the flameproofing solution is BEST applied to the fabric by _____ the fabric. 25.____
 A. sponging B. spraying C. dipping
 D. brushing E. sprinkling

KEY (CORRECT ANSWERS)

1.	B		11.	A
2.	B		12.	D
3.	D		13.	A
4.	C		14.	D
5.	A		15.	B
6.	C		16.	C
7.	A		17.	D
8.	D		18.	C
9.	B		19.	B
10.	A		20.	A

21. B
22. D
23. B
24. E
25. C

TEST 2

DIRECTIONS: All questions are to be answered SOLELY on the basis of the information contained in the passage. Each question or incomplete statement is followed by several suggested answers or completions. Select the one that BEST answers the question or completes the statement. *PRINT THE LETTER OF THE CORRECT ANSWER IN THE SPACE AT THE RIGHT.*

Questions 1-4.

Safety belts provide protection for the passengers of a vehicle by preventing them from crashing around inside if the vehicle is involved in a collision. They operate on the principle similar to that used in the packaging of fragile items. You become a part of the vehicle package and you are kept from being tossed about inside if the vehicle is suddenly decelerated. Many injury-causing collisions at low speeds—for example, at city intersections—could have been injury-free if the occupants had fastened their safety belts. There is a double advantage to the driver in that it not only protects him from harm, but prevents him from being yanked away from the wheel, thereby permitting him to maintain control of the car. Since, without seat belts, the risk of injury is about 50% greater, and the risk of death is about 30% greater, the State Vehicle and Traffic Law provided that a motor vehicle manufactured or assembled after June 30, 1964 and designated as a 1965 or later model should have two safety belts for the front seat. It also provides that a motor vehicle manufactured after June 30, 1966 and designated as a 1967 or later model should have at least one safety belt for the rear seat for each passenger for which the rear seat of such vehicle was designed.

1. The principle on which seat belts work is that
   A. a car and its driver and passengers are fragile
   B. a person fastened to the car will not be thrown around when the car slows down suddenly
   C. the driver and passengers of a car that is suddenly decelerated will be thrown forward
   D. the driver and passengers of an automobile should be packaged the way fragile items are packaged

1.____

2. We can assume from the above passage that safety belts should be worn at all times because you can never tell when
   A. a car will be forced to turn off onto another road
   B. it will be necessary to shift into low gear to go up a hill
   C. you will have to speed up to pass another car
   D. a car may have to come to a sudden stop

2.____

3. Besides preventing injury, an ADDITIONAL benefit from the use of safety belts is that
   A. collisions are fewer
   B. damage to the car is kept down
   C. the car can be kept under control
   D. the number of accidents at city intersections is reduced

3.____

4. The risk of death in car accidents for people who don't use safety belts is
   A. 30% greater than the risk of injury
   B. 30% greater than for those who do use them
   C. 50% less than the risk of injury
   D. 50% greater than for those who use them

Questions 5-9.

Any person who is living in New York City and is otherwise eligible may be granted public assistance whether or not he has New York State residence. However, since New York City does not contribute to the cost of assistance granted to persons who are without State residence, the cases of all recipients must be formally identified as to whether or not each member of the household has State residence.

To acquire State residence a person must have resided in New York State continuously for one year. Such residence is not lost unless the person is out of the State continuously for a period of one year or longer. Continuous residence does not include any period during which the individual is a patient in a hospital, an inmate of a public institution or of an incorporated private institution, a resident on a military reservation, or a minor residing in a boarding home while under the care of an authorized agency. Receipt of public assistance does not prevent a person from acquiring State residence. State residence, once acquired, is not lost because of absence from the State while a person is serving in the U.S. Armed Forces or the Merchant Marine; nor does a member of the family of such a person lose State residence while living with or near that person in these circumstances.

Each person, regardless of age, acquires or loses State residence as an individual. There is no derivative State residence except for an infant at the time of birth. He is deemed to have State residence if he is in the custody of both parents and either one of them has State residence, or if the parent having custody of him has State residence.

5. According to the above passage, an infant is deemed to have New York State residence at the time of his birth if
   A. he is born in New York State but neither of his parents is a resident
   B. he is in custody of only one parent, who is not a resident, but his other parent is a resident
   C. his brother and sister are residents
   D. he is in the custody of both his parents but only one of them is a resident

6. The Jones family consists of five members. Jack and Mary Jones have lived in New York State continuously for the past eighteen months after having lived in Ohio since they were born. Of their three children, one was born ten months ago and has been in custody of his parents since birth. Their second child lived in Ohio until six months ago and then moved in with his parents. Their third child had never lived in New York until he moved with his parents to New York eighteen months ago. However, he entered the armed forces one month later and has not lived in New York since that time.
   Based on the above passage, how many members of the Jones Family are New York State residents?
   A. 2   B. 3   C. 4   D. 5

7. Assuming that each of the following individuals has lived continuously in New York State for the past year and has never previously lived in the State, which one of them is a New York State resident?
   A. Jack Salinas, who has been an inmate in a State correctional facility for six months of the year
   B. Fran Johnson, who has lived on an Army base for the entire year
   C. Arlene Snyder, who married a non-resident during the past year
   D. Gary Phillips, who was a patient in a Veterans Administration hospital for the entire year

8. The above passage implies that the reason for determining whether or not a recipient of public assistance is a State resident is that
   A. the cost of assistance for non-residents is not a New York City responsibility
   B. non-residents living in New York City are not eligible for public assistance
   C. recipients of public assistance are barred from acquiring State residence
   D. New York City is responsible for the full cost of assistance to recipients who are residents

9. Assume that the Rollins household in New York City consists of six members at the present time—Anne Rollins, her three children, her aunt, and her uncle. Anne Rollins and one of her children moved to New York City seven months ago. Neither of them had previously lived in New York State. Her other two children have lived in New York City continuously for the past two years, as has her aunt. Anne Rollins' uncle had lived in New York City continuously for many years until two years ago. He then entered the armed forces and has returned to New York City within the past month.
   Based on the above passage, how many members of the Rollins' household are New York State residents?
   A. 2   B. 3   C. 4   D. 6

Questions 10-12.

The agreement under which a tenant rents property from a landlord is known as a lease. Generally speaking, leases are classified as either short-term or long-term in duration. They are further subdivided according to the method used to determine the amount of periodic rent payments. Of the many types of lease in use, the more commonly used ones are the following:
1. The straight or fixed lease is one in which rent may be paid in equal amounts throughout the duration of the lease. These are usually restricted to short-term leasing, or somewhat longer-term if clauses in the lease provide for periodic escalation of payments as the economy shifts.
2. Percentage leasing, used for short-term commercial leasing, provides the landlord with a stipulated percentage of a tenant's gross sales from goods and services sold on the premises, in addition to a fixed amount of rent.
3. The net lease, generally long-term (ten years or more), requires the tenant to pay all operating costs, including real estate taxes and insurance. In a net-net lease, the tenant further agrees to meet mortgage interest and principal payments.

4. An escalated lease, which is a long-term lease, requires rent to be of a stipulated base amount which periodically is subject to escalation in accordance with cost-of-living index scales, or in direct proportion to taxes, insurance, and operating costs.

10. Based on the information given in the above passage, which type of lease is MOST likely to be advantageous to a landlord if there is a high rate of inflation?
    A. Fixed lease
    B. Percentage lease
    C. Net lease
    D. Escalated lease

10.____

11. On the basis of the above passage, which type of lease would generally be MOST suitable for a well-established textile company which requires permanent facilities for its large operations?
    A. Percentage lease and escalated lease
    B. Escalated lease and net lease
    C. Straight lease and net lease
    D. Straight lease and percentage lease

11.____

12. According to the above passage, the only type of lease which assures the same amount of rent throughout a specified interval is the _____ lease.
    A. straight   B. percentage   C. net-net   D. escalated

12.____

Questions 13-18.

Basic to every office is the need for proper lighting. Inadequate lighting is a familiar cause of fatigue and serves to create a somewhat dismal atmosphere in the office. One requirement of proper lighting is that it be an appropriate intensity. Intensity is measured in foot-candles. According to the Illuminating Engineering Society of New York, for casual seeing tasks such as in reception rooms, inactive file rooms, and other service areas, it is recommended that the amount of light be 30 foot-candles. For ordinary seeing tasks such as reading and work in active file rooms and in mail rooms, the recommended lighting is 100 foot-candles. For very difficult seeing tasks such as accounting, transcribing, and business-machine use, the recommended lighting is 150 foot-candles.

Lighting intensity is only one requirement. Shadows and glare are to be avoided. For example, the larger the proportion of a ceiling filled with lighting units, the more glare-free and comfortable the lighting will be. Natural lighting from windows is not too dependable because on dark wintry days windows yield little usable light, and on sunny, summer afternoons the glare from windows may be very distracting. Desks should not face the windows. Finally, the main lighting source ought to be overhead and to the left of the user.

13. According to the above passage, insufficient light in the office may cause
    A. glare   B. shadows   C. tiredness   D. distraction

13.____

14. Based on the above passage, which of the following must be considered when planning lighting arrangements? The
    A. amount of natural light present
    B. amount of work to be done
    C. level of difficulty of work to be done
    D. type of activity to be carried out

14.____

15. It can be inferred from the above passage that a well-coordinated lighting scheme is likely to result in
    A. greater employee productivity
    B. elimination of light reflection
    C. lower lighting cost
    D. more use of natural light

16. Of the following, the BEST title for the above passage is:
    A. Characteristics of Light
    B. Light Measurement Devices
    C. Factors to Consider When Planning Lighting Systems
    D. Comfort vs. Cost When Devising Lighting Arrangements

17. According to the above passage, a foot-candle is a measurement of the
    A. number of bulbs used
    B. strength of the light
    C. contrast between glare and shadow
    D. proportion of the ceiling filled with lighting units

18. According to the above passage, the number of foot-candles of light that would be needed to copy figures onto a payroll is _____ foot-candles.
    A. less than 30   B. 350   C. 100   D. 140

Questions 19-22.

A summons is an official statement ordering a person to appear in court. In traffic violation situations, summonses are used when arrests need not be made. The main reason for traffic summonses is to deter motorists from repeating the same traffic violation. Occasionally, motorists may make unintentional driving errors and sometimes they are unaware of correct driving regulations. In cases such as these, the policy should be to have the Officer verbally inform the motorist of the violation and warn him against repeating it. The purpose of this practice is not to limit the number of summonses, but rather to prevent the issuing of summonses when the violation is not due to deliberate intent or to inexcusable negligence.

19. According to the above passage, the PRINCIPAL reason for issuing traffic summonses is to
    A. discourage motorists from violating these laws again
    B. increase the money collected by the city
    C. put traffic violators in prison
    D. have them serve as substitutes for police officers

20. The reason a verbal warning may sometimes be substituted for a summons is to
    A. limit the number of summonses
    B. distinguish between excusable and inexcusable violations
    C. provide harsher penalties for deliberate intent than for inexcusable negligence
    D. decrease the caseload in the courts

21. The author of the above passage feels that someone who violated a traffic regulation because he did not know about the regulation should be
    A. put under arrest
    B. fined less money
    C. given a summons
    D. told not to do it again

22. Using the distinctions made by the author of the above passage, the one of the following motorists to whom it would be MOST desirable to issue a summons is the one who exceeded the speed limit because he
    A. did not know the speed limit
    B. was late for an important business appointment
    C. speeded to avoid being hit by another car
    D. had a speedometer which was not working properly

Questions 24-25.

Physical design plays a very significant role in crime rate. Crime rate has been found to increase almost proportionately with building height. The average number of crimes is much greater in higher buildings than in lower ones (equal to or less than six stories). What is most interesting is that in buildings of six stories or less, the project size or total number of units does not make a difference. It seems that, although larger projects encourage crime by fostering feelings of anonymity, isolation, irresponsibility, and lack of identity with surroundings, evidence indicate that larger projects encompassed in low buildings seem to offset what we may assume to be factors conducive to high crime rates. High-rise projects not only experience a higher rate of crime within the buildings, but a greater proportion of the crime occurs in the interior public spaces of these buildings as compared with those of the lower buildings. Lower buildings have more limited public space than higher ones. A criminal probably perceives that the interior public areas of buildings are where his victims are most vulnerable and where the possibility of his being seen or apprehended is minimal. Placement of elevators, entrance lobbies, and secondary exits all are factors related to the likelihood of crimes taking place in buildings. The study of all of these elements should bear some weight in the planning of new projects.

23. According to the above passage, which of the following BEST describes the relationship between building size and crime?
    A. Larger projects lead to a greater crime rate.
    B. Higher buildings tend to increase the crime rate.
    C. The smaller the number of project apartments in low buildings the higher the crime rate
    D. Anonymity and isolation serve to lower the crime rate in small buildings.

24. According to the above passage, the likelihood of a criminal attempting a mugging in the interior public portions of a high-rise building is good because
    A. tenants will be constantly flowing in and out of the area
    B. there is easy access to fire stairs and secondary exits
    C. there is a good chance that no one will see him
    D. tenants may not recognize the victims of crime as their neighbors

25. Which of the following is *implied* by the above passage as an explanation for the fact that the crime rate is lower in large low-rise housing projects than in large high-rise projects?
    A. Tenants know each other better and take a greater interest in what happens in the project.
    B. There is more public space where tenants are likely to gather together.
    C. The total number of units in a low-rise project is fewer than the total number of units in a high-rise project.
    D. Elevators in low-rise buildings travel quickly, thus limiting the amount of time in which a criminal can act.

KEY (CORRECT ANSWERS)

1.	B		11.	B
2.	D		12.	A
3.	C		13.	C
4.	B		14.	D
5.	D		15.	A
6.	B		16.	C
7.	C		17.	B
8.	A		18.	D
9.	C		19.	A
10.	D		20.	B

21.	D
22.	B
23.	B
24.	C
25.	A

READING COMPREHENSION
UNDERSTANDING WRITTEN MATERIALS

COMMENTARY

The ability to read and understand written materials—texts, publications, newspapers, orders, directions, expositions—is a skill basic to a functioning democracy and to an efficient business or viable government.

That is why almost all examinations—for beginning, middle, and senior levels—test reading comprehension, directly or indirectly.

The reading test measures how well you understand what you read. This is how it is done: You read a passage followed by several statements. From these statements, you choose the one statement, or answer, that is BEST supported by, or BEST matches, what is said in the paragraph. PRINT THE LETTER OF THE CORRECT ANSWER IN THE SPACE AT THE RIGHT.

SAMPLE QUESTION

DIRECTIONS: Answer Question 1 ONLY according to the information given in the following passage.

1. A cashier has to make many arithmetic calculations in connection with his work. Skill in arithmetic comes readily with practice; no special talent is needed.
   On the basis of the above statement, it is MOST accurate to state that
   A. the most important part of a cashier's job is to make calculations
   B. few cashiers have the special ability needed to handle arithmetic problems easily
   C. without special talent, cashiers cannot learn to do the calculations they are required to do in their work
   D. a cashier can, with practice, learn to handle the computations he is required to make

1.____

The CORRECT answer is D.

EXAMINATION SECTION
TEST 1

DIRECTIONS: Questions 1 through 5 are to be answered on the basis of the following reading passage. *PRINT THE LETTER OF THE CORRECT ANSWER IN THE SPACE AT THE RIGHT.*

The size of each collection route will be determined by the amount of waste per stop, distance between stops, speed of loading, speed of truck, traffic conditions during loading time, etc.

Basically, the route should consist of a proper amount of work for a crew for the daily work period. The crew should service all properties eligible for this service in their area. Routes should, whenever practical, be compact, with a logical progression through the area. Unnecessary travel should be avoided. Traffic conditions on the route should be thoroughly studied to prevent lost time in loading, to reduce hazards to employees, and to minimize tying up of regular traffic movements by collection forces. Natural and physical barriers and arterial streets should be used as route boundaries wherever possible to avoid lost time in travel.

Routes within a district should be laid out so that the crews start at the point farthest from the disposal area and, as the day progresses, move toward that area, thus reducing the length of the haul. When possible, the work of the crews in a district should be parallel as they progress throughout the day, with routes finishing up within a short distance of each other. This enables the supervisor to be present when crews are completing their work and enables him to shift crews to trouble spots to complete the day's work.

1. Based on the above passage, an advantage of having collection routes end near one another is that
    A. routes can be made more compact
    B. unnecessary travel is avoided, saving manpower
    C. the length of the haul is reduced
    D. the supervisor can exercise better manpower control

2. Of the factors mentioned above which affect the size of a collection route, the two over which the sanitation forces have LEAST control are
    A. amount of waste; traffic conditions
    B. speed of loading; amount of waste
    C. speed of truck; distance between stops
    D. traffic conditions; speed of truck

3. According to the above passage, the size of a collection route is probably good if
    A. it is a fair day's work for a normal crew
    B. it is not necessary for the trucks to travel too fast
    C. the amount of waste collected can be handled properly
    D. the distance between stops is approximately equal

4. Based on the above passage, it is reasonable to assume that a sanitation officer laying out collection routes should NOT try to have
   A. an arterial street as a route boundary
   B. any routes near the disposal area
   C. the routes overlap a little
   D. the routes run in the same direction

5. The term "logical progression," as used in the second paragraph of the passage refers MOST NEARLY to
   A. collecting from street after street in order
   B. numbering streets one after the other
   C. rotating crew assignments
   D. using logic as a basis for assigned crews

KEY (CORRECT ANSWERS)

1. D
2. A
3. A
4. C
5. A

TEST 2

DIRECTIONS: Questions 1 through 3 are to be answered on the basis of the following reading passage. *PRINT THE LETTER OF THE CORRECT ANSWER IN THE SPACE AT THE RIGHT.*

In an open discussion designed to arrive at solutions to community problems, the person leading the discussion group should give the members a chance to make their suggestions before he makes his. He must not be afraid of silence; if he talks just to keep things going, he will find he can't stop, and good discussion will not develop. In other words, the more he talks, the more the group will depend on him. If he finds, however, that no one seems ready to begin the discussion, his best "opening" is to ask for definitions of terms which form the basis of the discussion. By pulling out as many definitions or interpretations as possible, he can get the group started "thinking out load," which is essential to good discussion.

1. According to the above passage, good group discussion is MOST likely to result if the person leading the discussion group
   A. keeps the discussion going by speaking whenever the group stops speaking
   B. encourages the group to depend on him by speaking more than any other group member
   C. makes his own suggestions before the group has a chance to make theirs
   D. encourages discussion by asking the group to interpret the terms to be discussed

1.____

2. According to the above passage, "thinking out loud" by the discussion group is
   A. *good* practice, because "thinking out loud" is important to good discussion
   B. *poor* practice, because group members should think out their ideas before discussing them
   C. *good* practice, because it will encourage the person leading the discussion to speak more
   D. *poor* practice, because it causes the group to fear silence during discussion

2.____

3. According to the above passage, the one of the following which is LEAST desirable at an open discussion is having
   A. silent periods during which none of the group members speaks
   B. differences of opinion among the group members concerning the definition of terms
   C. a discussion leader who uses "openings" to get the discussion started
   D. a discussion leader who provides all suggestions and definitions for the group

3.____

KEY (CORRECT ANSWERS)

1. D
2. A
3. D

TEST 3

DIRECTIONS: Questions 1 through 4 are to be answered on the basis of the following reading passage. *PRINT THE LETTER OF THE CORRECT ANSWER IN THE SPACE AT THE RIGHT.*

The insects you will control are just a minute fraction of the millions which inhabit the world. Man does well to hold his own in the face of the constant pressures that insects continue to exert upon him. Not only are the total numbers tremendous, but the number of individual kinds, or species, certainly exceeds 800,000—number greater than that of all other animals combined. Many of these are beneficial but some are especially competitive with man. Not only are insects numerous, but they are among the most adaptable of all animals. In their many forms, they are fitted for almost any specific way of life. Their adaptability, combined with their tremendous rate of reproduction, gives insects an unequaled potential for survival!

The food of insects includes almost anything that can be eaten by any other animal as well as many things which cannot even be digested by any other animals. Most insects do not harm the products of man or carry diseases harmful to him; however, many do carry diseases and others feed on his food and manufactured goods. Some are adapted to living only in open areas while others are able to live in extremely confined spaces. All of these factor combined make the insects a group of animals having many members which are a nuisance to man and thus of great importance.

The control of insects requires an understanding of their way of life. Thus, it is necessary to understand the anatomy of the insect, its method of growth, the time it takes for the insect to grow from egg to adult, its habits, the stage of its life history in which it causes damage, its food, and its common living places. In order to obtain the best control, it is especially important to be able to identify correctly the specific insect involved because, without this knowledge, it is impossible to prescribe a proper treatment.

1. Which one of the following is a CORRECT statement about the insect population of the world, according to the above passage? The
   A. total number of insects is less than the total number of all other animals combined
   B. number of species of insects is greater than the number of species of all other animals combined
   C. total number of harmful insects is less than the number of species of those which are harmful
   D. number of species of harmless insects is less than the number of species of those which are harmful

1.____

2. Insects will be controlled MOST efficiently if you
   A. understand why the insects are so numerous
   B. know what insects you are dealing with
   C. see if the insects compete with man
   D. are able to identify the food which the insects digest

2.____

3. According to the above passage, insects are of importance to a scientist PRIMARILY because they
   A. can be annoying, destructive, and harmful to man
   B. are able to thrive in very small spaces
   C. cause damage during their growth stages
   D. are so adaptable that they can adjust to any environment

4. According to the above passage, insects can eat
   A. everything that any other living thing can eat
   B. man's food and thing which he makes
   C. anything which other animals can't digest
   D. only food and food products

KEY (CORRECT ANSWERS)

1. B
2. B
3. A
4. B

TEST 4

DIRECTIONS: Questions 1 through 3 are to be answered on the basis of the following reading passage. *PRINT THE LETTER OF THE CORRECT ANSWER IN THE SPACE AT THE RIGHT.*

Telephone service in a government agency should be adequate and complete with respect to information given or action taken. It must be remembered that telephone contacts should receive special consideration since the caller cannot see the operator. People like to feel that they are receiving personal attention and that their requests or criticisms are receiving individual rather than routine consideration. All this contributes to what has come to be known as *tone of service*. The aim is to use standards which are clearly very good or superior. The factors to be considered in determining what makes good tone of service are speech, courtesy, understanding, and explanations. A caller's impression of tone of service will affect the general public attitude toward the agency and city services in general.

1. The above passage states that people who telephone a government agency like to feel that they are
   A. creating a positive image of themselves
   B. being given routine consideration
   C. receiving individual attention
   D. setting standards for telephone service

2. Which one of the following is NOT mentioned in the above passage as a factor in determining good tone of service?
   A. Courtesy   B. Education   C. Speech   D. Understanding

3. The above passage implies that failure to properly handle telephone calls is MOST likely to result in
   A. a poor impression of city agencies by the public
   B. a deterioration of courtesy toward operators
   C. an effort by operators to improve the Tone of Service
   D. special consideration by the public of operator difficulties

KEY (CORRECT ANSWERS)

1. C
2. B
3. A

TEST 5

DIRECTIONS: Questions 1 through 5 are to be answered on the basis of the following reading passage. *PRINT THE LETTER OF THE CORRECT ANSWER IN THE SPACE AT THE RIGHT.*

For some office workers it is useful to be familiar with the four main classes of domestic mail; for others, it is essential. Each class has a different rate of postage and some have requirements concerning wrapping, sealing, or special information to be placed on the package.

First-class mail, the class which may not be opened for postal inspection, includes letters, postcards, business reply cards, and other kinds of written matter. There are different rates for some of the kinds of cards which can be sent by first-class mail. The maximum weight for an item sent by first-class mail is 70 pounds. An item which is not letter size should be marked "First Class: on all sides.

Although office workers most often come into contact with first-class mail, they may find it helpful to know something about the other classes. Second-class mail is generally used for mailing newspapers and magazines. Publishers of these articles must meet certain U.S. Postal Service requirements in order to obtain a permit to use second-class mailing rates. Third-class mail, which must weigh less than 1 pound, includes printed materials and merchandise parcels. There are two rate structure for this class, a single-piece rate and a bulk rate. Fourth-class mail, also known as parcel post, includes packages weighing from one to 40 pounds. For more information about these classes of mail and the actual mailing rates, contact our local post office.

1. According to this passage, first-class mail is the only class which 1.____
   A. has a limit on the maximum weight of an item
   B. has different rates for items within the class
   C. may not be opened for postal inspection
   D. should be used by office workers

2. According to this passage, the one of the following items which may CORRECTLY 2.____
   be sent by fourth-class mail is a
   A. magazine weighing one-half pound
   B. package weighing one-half pound
   C. package weighing two pounds
   D. postcard

3. According to this passage, there are different postage rates for 3.____
   A. a newspaper sent by second-class mail and a magazine sent by second-class mail
   B. each of the classes of mail
   C. each pound of fourth-class mail
   D. printed material sent by third-class mail and merchandise parcels sent by third-class mail

4. In order to send a newspaper by second-class mail, a publisher must 4._____
   A. have met certain postal requirements and obtained a permit
   B. indicate whether he wants to use the single-piece or the bulk rate
   C. make certain that the newspaper weighs less than one pound
   D. mark the newspaper "Second Class" on the top and bottom of the wrapper

5. Of the following types of information, the one which is NOT mentioned in the passage is the 5._____
   A. class of mail to which parcel post belongs
   B. kinds of items which can be sent by each class of mail
   C. maximum weight for an item sent by fourth-class mail
   D. postage rate for each of the four classes of mail

KEY (CORRECT ANSWERS)

1. C
2. C
3. B
4. A
5. D

TEST 6

DIRECTIONS: Questions 1 through 5 are to be answered on the basis of the following reading passage. *PRINT THE LETTER OF THE CORRECT ANSWER IN THE SPACE AT THE RIGHT.*

The thickness of insulation necessary for the most economical results varies with the steam temperature. The standard covering consists of 85 percent magnesia with 10 percent of long-fibre asbestos as a binder. Both magnesia and laminated asbestos-felt and other forms of mineral wool including glass wool are also used for heat insulation. The magnesia and laminated-asbestos coverings may be safely used at temperatures up to 600°F. Pipe insulation is applied in molded sections 3 feet long; the sections are attached to the pipe by means of galvanized iron wire or netting. Flanges and fittings can be insulated by direct application of magnesia cement to the metal without *reinforcement*. Insulation should always be maintained inn good condition because it saves fuel. Routine maintenance of warm-pipe insulation should include prompt repair of damaged surfaces. Steam and hot-water leaks concealed by insulation will be difficult to detect. Underground steam or hot-water pipes are best insulated using a concrete trench with removable cover.

1. The word *reinforcement*, as used above, means MOST NEARLY 1.____
   A. resistance   B. strengthening
   C. regulation   D. removal

2. According to the above paragraph, magnesia and laminated asbestos 2.____
   coverings may be safely used at temperatures up to
   A. 800°F   B. 720°F   C. 675°F   D. 600°F

3. According to the above paragraph, insulation should *always* be maintained 3.____
   in good condition because it
   A. is laminated   B. saves fuel
   C. is attached to the pipe   D. prevents leaks

4. According to the above paragraph, pipe insulation sections are attached to the 4.____
   pipe by means of
   A. binders   B. mineral wool
   C. netting   D. staples

5. According to the above paragraph, a leak in a hot-water pipe may be difficult 5.____
   to detect because, when insulation is used, the leak is
   A. underground   B. hidden   C. routine   D. cemented

KEY (CORRECT ANSWERS)

1. B
2. D
3. B
4. C
5. B

TEST 7

DIRECTIONS: Questions 1 through 4 are to be answered on the basis of the following reading passage. *PRINT THE LETTER OF THE CORRECT ANSWER IN THE SPACE AT THE RIGHT.*

Cylindrical surfaces are the most common form of finished surfaces found on machine parts, although flat surfaces are also very common; hence, many metal-cutting processes are for the purpose of producing either cylindrical or flat surfaces. The machines used for cylindrical or flat shapes may be, and often are, utilized also for forming the various irregular or special shapes required on many machine parts. Because of the prevalence of cylindrical and flat surfaces, the student of manufacturing practice should learn first about the machines and methods employed to produce these surfaces. The cylindrical surfaces may be internal as in holes and cylinders. Any one part may, of course, have cylindrical sections of different diameters and lengths and include flat ends or shoulders and, frequently, there is a threaded part or, possibly, some finished surface that is not circular in cross-section. The prevalence of cylindrical surfaces on machine parts explains why lathes are found in all machine shops. It is important to understand the various uses of the lathes because many of the operations are the same fundamentally as those performed on other types of machine tools.

1. According to the above passage, the MOST common form of finished surfaces found on machine parts is
   A. cylindrical   B. elliptical   C. flat   D. square

2. According to the above passage, any one part of cylindrical surfaces may have
   A. chases   B. shoulders   C. keyways   D. splines

3. According to the above passage, lathes are found in all machine shops because cylindrical surfaces on machine parts are
   A. scarce   B. internal   C. common   D. external

4. As used in the above paragraph, the word *processes* means
   A. operations   B. purposes   C. devices   D. tools

KEY (CORRECT ANSWERS)

1. A
2. B
3. C
4. A

TEST 8

DIRECTIONS: Questions 1 and 2 are to be answered on the basis of the following reading passage. *PRINT THE LETTER OF THE CORRECT ANSWER IN THE SPACE AT THE RIGHT.*

The principle of interchangeability requires manufacture to such specification that component parts of a device may be selected at random and assembled to fit and operate satisfactorily. Interchangeable manufacture, therefore, requires that parts be made to definite limits of error, and to fit gages instead of mating parts. Interchangeability does not necessarily involve a high degree of precision; stove lids, for example, are interchangeable but are not particularly accurate, and carriage bolts and nuts are not precision products but are completely interchangeable. Interchangeability may be employed in unit-production as well as mass-production systems of manufacture.

1. According to the above paragraph, in order for parts to be interchangeable, they must be
   A. precision-machined
   B. selectively-assembled
   C. mass-produced
   D. made to fit gages

   1.____

2. According to the above paragraph, carriage bolts are interchangeable because they are
   A. precision-made
   B. sized to specific tolerances
   C. individually matched products
   D. produced in small units

   2.____

KEY (CORRECT ANSWERS)

1. D
2. B

EXAMINATION SECTION
TEST 1

DIRECTIONS: Each question or incomplete statement is followed by several suggested answers or completions. Select the one that BEST answers the question or completes the statement. *PRINT THE LETTER OF THE CORRECT ANSWER IN THE SPACE AT THE RIGHT.*

Questions 1-50.

DIRECTIONS: Each of Questions 1 through 50 consists of a word in capital letters followed by four suggested meanings of the word. For each question, choose the word or phrase which means MOST NEARLY the same as the word in capital letters.

1. ABUT
   A. abandon B. assist C. border on D. renounce

2. ABSCOND
   A. draw in B. give up
   C. refrain from D. deal off

3. BEQUEATH
   A. deaden B. hand down C. make sad D. scold

4. BOGUS
   A. sad B. false C. shocking D. stolen

5. CALAMITY
   A. disaster B. female C. insanity D. patriot

6. COMPULSORY
   A. binding B. ordinary C. protected D. ruling

7. CONSIGN
   A. agree with B. benefit
   C. commit D. drive down

8. DEBILITY
   A. failure B. legality
   C. quality D. weakness

9. DEFRAUD
   A. cheat B. deny
   C. reveal D. tie

10. DEPOSITION
    A. absence B. publication
    C. removal D. testimony

11. DOMICILE
    A. anger B. dwelling
    C. tame D. willing

12. HEARSAY
    A. selfish   B. serious   C. rumor   D. unlikely

13. HOMOGENEOUS
    A. human   B. racial   C. similar   D. unwise

14. ILLICIT
    A. understood   B. uneven   C. unkind   D. unlawful

15. LEDGER
    A. book of accounts   B. editor
    C. periodical   D. shelf

16. NARRATIVE
    A. gossip   B. natural   C. negative   D. story

17. PLAUSIBLE
    A. reasonable   B. respectful   C. responsible   D. rightful

18. RECIPIENT
    A. absentee   B. receiver   C. speaker   D. substitute

19. SUBSTANTIATE
    A. appear for   B. arrange
    C. confirm   D. combine

20. SURMISE
    A. aim   B. break   C. guess   D. order

21. ALTER EGO
    A. business partner   B. confidential friend
    C. guide   D. subconscious conflict

22. FOURTH ESTATE
    A. the aristocracy   B. the clergy
    C. the judiciary   D. the newspapers

23. IMPEACH
    A. accuse   B. find guilty
    C. remove   D. try

24. PROPENSITY
    A. dislike   B. helpfulness
    C. inclination   D. supervision

25. SPLENETIC
    A. charming   B. peevish   C. shining   D. sluggish

26. SUBORN
    A. bribe someone to commit perjury
    B. demote someone several levels in rank
    C. deride
    D. substitute

27. TALISMAN
    A. charm
    B. juror
    C. prayer shawl
    D. native

28. VITREOUS
    A. corroding
    B. glassy
    C. nourishing
    D. sticky

29. WRY
    A. comic
    B. grained
    C. resilient
    D. twisted

30. SIGNATORY
    A. lawyer who draws up a legal document
    B. document that must be signed by a judge
    C. person who signs a document
    D. true copy of a signature

31. RETAINER
    A. fee paid to a lawyer for his services
    B. document held by a third party
    C. court decision to send a prisoner back to custody pending trial
    D. legal requirement to keep certain types of files

32. BEQUEATH
    A. to receive assistance from a charitable organization
    B. to give personal property by will to another
    C. to transfer real property from one person to another
    D. to receive an inheritance upon the death of a relative

33. RATIFY
    A. approve and sanction
    B. forego
    C. produce evidence
    D. summarize

34. CODICIL
    A. document introduced in evidence in a civil action
    B. subsection of a law
    C. type of legal action that can be brought by a plaintiff
    D. supplement or an addition to a will

35. ALIAS
    A. assumed name
    B. in favor of
    C. against
    D. a writ

36. PROXY
    A. a phony document in a real estate transaction
    B. an opinion by a judge of a civil court
    C. a document containing appointment of an agent
    D. a summons in a lawsuit

37. ALLEGED
    A. innocent
    B. asserted
    C. guilty
    D. called upon

38. EXECUTE
    A. to complete a legal document by signing it
    B. to set requirements
    C. to render services to a duly elected executive of a municipality
    D. to initiate legal action such as a lawsuit

39. NOTARY PUBLIC
    A. lawyer who is running for public office
    B. judge who hears minor cases
    C. public officer, one of whose functions is to administer oaths
    D. lawyer who gives free legal services to persons unable to pay

40. WAIVE
    A. to disturb a calm state of affairs
    B. to knowingly renounce a right or claim
    C. to pardon someone for a minor fault
    D. to purposely mislead a person during an investigation

41. ARRAIGN
    A. to prevent an escape
    B. to defend a prisoner
    C. to verify a document
    D. to accuse in a court of law

42. VOLUNTARY
    A. by free choice   B. necessary
    C. important   D. by design

43. INJUNCTION
    A. act of prohibiting   B. process of inserting
    C. means of arbitrating   D. freedom of action

44. AMICABLE
    A. compelled   B. friendly
    C. unimportant   D. insignificant

45. CLOSED SHOP
    A. one that employs only members of a union
    B. one that employs union members and unaffiliated employees
    C. one that employs only employees with previous experience
    D. one that employs skilled and unskilled workers

46. ABDUCT
    A. lead   B. kidnap   C. sudden   D. worthless

47. BIAS
    A. ability   B. envy   C. prejudice   D. privilege

48. COERCE
    A. cancel   B. force   C. rescind   D. rugged

49. CONDONE
    A. combine   B. pardon   C. revive   D. spice

50. CONSISTENCY
    A. bravery
    C. strain
    B. readiness
    D. uniformity

KEY (CORRECT ANSWERS)

1. C	11. B	21. B	31. A	41. D
2. D	12. C	22. D	32. B	42. A
3. B	13. C	23. A	33. A	43. A
4. B	14. D	24. C	34. D	44. B
5. A	15. A	25. B	35. A	45. A
6. A	16. D	26. A	36. C	46. B
7. C	17. A	27. A	37. B	47. C
8. D	18. B	28. B	38. A	48. B
9. A	19. C	29. D	39. C	49. B
10. D	20. C	30. C	40. B	50. D

TEST 2

DIRECTIONS: Each question or incomplete statement is followed by several suggested answers or completions. Select the one that BEST answers the question or completes the statement. *PRINT THE LETTER OF THE CORRECT ANSWER IN THE SPACE AT THE RIGHT.*

1. In the sentence, *The prisoner was fractious when brought to the station house*, the word *fractious* means MOST NEARLY
   A. penitent
   B. talkative
   C. irascible
   D. broken-hearted

1.___

2. In the sentence, *The judge was implacable when the attorney pleaded for leniency*, the word *implacable* means MOST NEARLY
   A. inexorable
   B. disinterested
   C. inattentive
   D. indifferent

2.___

3. In the sentence, *The court ordered the mendacious statements stricken from the record*, the word *mendacious* means MOST NEARLY
   A. begging
   B. lying
   C. threatening
   D. lengthy

3.___

4. In the sentence, *The district attorney spoke in a strident voice*, the word *strident* means MOST NEARLY
   A. loud
   B. harsh-sounding
   C. sing-song
   D. low

4.___

5. In the sentence, *The speaker had a predilection for long sentences*, the word *predilection* means MOST NEARLY
   A. aversion
   B. talent
   C. propensity
   D. diffidence

5.___

6. A person who has an uncontrollable desire to steal without need is called a
   A. dipsomaniac
   B. kleptomaniac
   C. monomaniac
   D. pyromaniac

6.___

7. In the sentence, *Malice was immanent in all his remarks*, the word *immanent* means MOST NEARLY
   A. elevated
   B. inherent
   C. threatening
   D. foreign

7.___

8. In the sentence, *The extant copies of the document were found in the safe*, the word *extant* means MOST NEARLY
   A. existing
   B. original
   C. forged
   D. duplicate

8.___

9. In the sentence, *The recruit was more complaisant after the captain spoke to him*, the word *complaisant* means MOST NEARLY
   A. calm
   B. affable
   C. irritable
   D. confident

9.___

10. In the sentence, *The man was captured under highly creditable circumstances*, the word *creditable* means MOST NEARLY
    A. doubtful
    B. believable
    C. praiseworthy
    D. unexpected

11. In the sentence, *His superior officers were more sagacious than he*, the word *sagacious* means MOST NEARLY
    A. shrewd
    B. obtuse
    C. absurd
    D. verbose

12. In the sentence, *He spoke with impunity*, the word *impunity* means MOST NEARLY
    A. rashness
    B. caution
    C. without fear
    D. immunity

13. In the sentence, *The new officer displayed unusual temerity during the emergency*, the word *temerity* means MOST NEARLY
    A. fear
    B. rashness
    C. calmness
    D. anxiety

14. In the sentence, *The portions of food were parsimoniously served*, the word *parsimoniously* means MOST NEARLY
    A. stingily
    B. piously
    C. elaborately
    D. generously

15. In the sentence, *Generally the speaker's remarks were sententious*, the word *sententious* means MOST NEARLY
    A. verbose
    B. witty
    C. argumentative
    D. pithy

Questions 16-20.

DIRECTIONS: Next to the number which corresponds with the number of each item in Column I, place the letter preceding the adjective in Column II which BEST describes the persons in Column I.

COLUMN I		COLUMN II
16. Talkative woman	A.	abstemious
17. Person on a reducing diet	B.	pompous
18. Scholarly professor	C.	erudite
19. Man who seldom speaks	D.	benevolent
20. Charitable person	E.	docile
	F.	loquacious
	G.	indefatigable
	H.	taciturn

Questions 21-25.

DIRECTIONS: Next to the number which corresponds with the number preceding each profession in Column I, place the letter preceding the word in Column II which BEST explains the subject matter of that profession.

COLUMN I		COLUMN II	
21.	Geologist	A.	animals
22.	Oculist	B.	eyes
23.	Podiatrist	C.	feet
24.	Palmist	D.	fortune-telling
25.	Zoologist	E.	language
		F.	rocks
		G.	stamps
		H.	woman

Questions 26-30.

DIRECTIONS: Next to the number corresponding to the number of each of the words in Column I, place the letter preceding the word in Column II that is MOST NEARLY OPPOSITE to it in meaning.

COLUMN I		COLUMN II	
26.	comely	A.	beautiful
27.	eminent	B.	cowardly
28.	frugal	C.	kind
29.	gullible	D.	sedate
30.	valiant	E.	shrewd
		F.	ugly
		G.	unknown
		H.	wasteful

KEY (CORRECT ANSWERS)

1.	C	11.	A	21.	F
2.	A	12.	D	22.	B
3.	B	13.	B	23.	C
4.	B	14.	A	24.	D
5.	C	15.	D	25.	A
6.	B	16.	F	26.	F
7.	B	17.	A	27.	G
8.	A	18.	C	28.	H
9.	B	19.	H	29.	E
10.	C	20.	D	30.	B

GLOSSARY OF LEGAL TERMS

TABLE OF CONTENTS

	Page
Action ... Affiant	1
Affidavit ... At Bar	2
At Issue ... Burden of Proof	3
Business ... Commute	4
Complainant ... Conviction	5
Cooperative ... Demur (v.)	6
Demurrage ... Endorsement	7
Enjoin ... Facsimile	8
Factor ... Guilty	9
Habeas Corpus ... Incumbrance	10
Indemnify ... Laches	11
Landlord and Tenant ... Malice	12
Mandamus ... Obiter Dictum	13
Object (v.) ... Perjury	14
Perpetuity ... Proclamation	15
Proffered Evidence ... Referee	16
Referendum ... Stare Decisis	17
State ... Term	18
Testamentary ... Warrant (Warranty) (v.)	19
Warrant (n.) ... Zoning	20

GLOSSARY OF LEGAL TERMS

A

ACTION - "Action" includes a civil action and a criminal action.
A FORTIORI - A term meaning you can reason one thing from the existence of certain facts.
A POSTERIORI - From what goes after; from effect to cause.
A PRIORI - From what goes before; from cause to effect.
AB INITIO - From the beginning.
ABATE - To diminish or put an end to.
ABET - To encourage the commission of a crime.
ABEYANCE - Suspension, temporary suppression.
ABIDE - To accept the consequences of.
ABJURE - To renounce; give up.
ABRIDGE - To reduce; contract; diminish.
ABROGATE - To annul, repeal, or destroy.
ABSCOND - To hide or absent oneself to avoid legal action.
ABSTRACT - A summary.
ABUT - To border on, to touch.
ACCESS - Approach; in real property law it means the right of the owner of property to the use of the highway or road next to his land, without obstruction by intervening property owners.
ACCESSORY - In criminal law, it means the person who contributes or aids in the commission of a crime.
ACCOMMODATED PARTY - One to whom credit is extended on the strength of another person signing a commercial paper.
ACCOMMODATION PAPER - A commercial paper to which the accommodating party has put his name.
ACCOMPLICE - In criminal law, it means a person who together with the principal offender commits a crime.
ACCORD - An agreement to accept something different or less than that to which one is entitled, which extinguishes the entire obligation.
ACCOUNT - A statement of mutual demands in the nature of debt and credit between parties.
ACCRETION - The act of adding to a thing; in real property law, it means gradual accumulation of land by natural causes.
ACCRUE - To grow to; to be added to.
ACKNOWLEDGMENT - The act of going before an official authorized to take acknowledgments, and acknowledging an act as one's own.
ACQUIESCENCE - A silent appearance of consent.
ACQUIT - To legally determine the innocence of one charged with a crime.
AD INFINITUM - Indefinitely.
AD LITEM - For the suit.
AD VALOREM - According to value.
ADJECTIVE LAW - Rules of procedure.
ADJUDICATION - The judgment given in a case.
ADMIRALTY - Court having jurisdiction over maritime cases.
ADULT - Sixteen years old or over (in criminal law).
ADVANCE - In commercial law, it means to pay money or render other value before it is due.
ADVERSE - Opposed; contrary.
ADVOCATE - (v.) To speak in favor of;
(n.) One who assists, defends, or pleads for another.
AFFIANT - A person who makes and signs an affidavit.

AFFIDAVIT - A written and sworn to declaration of facts, voluntarily made.

AFFINITY - The relationship between persons through marriage with the kindred of each other; distinguished from consanguinity, which is the relationship by blood.

AFFIRM - To ratify; also when an appellate court affirms a judgment, decree, or order, it means that it is valid and right and must stand as rendered in the lower court.

AFOREMENTIONED; AFORESAID - Before or already said.

AGENT - One who represents and acts for another.

AID AND COMFORT - To help; encourage.

ALIAS - A name not one's true name.

ALIBI - A claim of not being present at a certain place at a certain time.

ALLEGE - To assert.

ALLOTMENT - A share or portion.

AMBIGUITY - Uncertainty; capable of being understood in more than one way.

AMENDMENT - Any language made or proposed as a change in some principal writing.

AMICUS CURIAE - A friend of the court; one who has an interest in a case, although not a party in the case, who volunteers advice upon matters of law to the judge. For example, a brief amicus curiae.

AMORTIZATION - To provide for a gradual extinction of (a future obligation) in advance of maturity, especially, by periodical contributions to a sinking fund which will be adequate to discharge a debt or make a replacement when it becomes necessary.

ANCILLARY - Aiding, auxiliary.

ANNOTATION - A note added by way of comment or explanation.

ANSWER - A written statement made by a defendant setting forth the grounds of his defense.

ANTE - Before.

ANTE MORTEM - Before death.

APPEAL - The removal of a case from a lower court to one of superior jurisdiction for the purpose of obtaining a review.

APPEARANCE - Coming into court as a party to a suit.

APPELLANT - The party who takes an appeal from one court or jurisdiction to another (appellate) court for review.

APPELLEE - The party against whom an appeal is taken.

APPROPRIATE - To make a thing one's own.

APPROPRIATION - Prescribing the destination of a thing; the act of the legislature designating a particular fund, to be applied to some object of government expenditure.

APPURTENANT - Belonging to; accessory or incident to.

ARBITER - One who decides a dispute; a referee.

ARBITRARY - Unreasoned; not governed by any fixed rules or standard.

ARGUENDO - By way of argument.

ARRAIGN - To call the prisoner before the court to answer to a charge.

ASSENT - A declaration of willingness to do something in compliance with a request.

ASSERT - Declare.

ASSESS - To fix the rate or amount.

ASSIGN - To transfer; to appoint; to select for a particular purpose.

ASSIGNEE - One who receives an assignment.

ASSIGNOR - One who makes an assignment.

AT BAR - Before the court.

AT ISSUE - When parties in an action come to a point where one asserts something and the other denies it.
ATTACH - Seize property by court order and sometimes arrest a person.
ATTEST - To witness a will, etc.; act of attestation.
AVERMENT - A positive statement of facts.

B

BAIL - To obtain the release of a person from legal custody by giving security and promising that he shall appear in court; to deliver (goods, etc.) in trust to a person for a special purpose.
BAILEE - One to whom personal property is delivered under a contract of bailment.
BAILMENT - Delivery of personal property to another to be held for a certain purpose and to be returned when the purpose is accomplished.
BAILOR - The party who delivers goods to another, under a contract of bailment.
BANC (OR BANK) - Bench; the place where a court sits permanently or regularly; also the assembly of all the judges of a court.
BANKRUPT - An insolvent person, technically, one declared to be bankupt after a bankruptcy proceeding.
BAR - The legal profession.
BARRATRY - Exciting groundless judicial proceedings.
BARTER - A contract by which parties exchange goods for other goods.
BATTERY - Illegal interfering with another's person.
BEARER - In commercial law, it means the person in possession of a commercial paper which is payable to the bearer.
BENCH - The court itself or the judge.
BENEFICIARY - A person benefiting under a will, trust, or agreement.
BEST EVIDENCE RULE,THE - Except as otherwise provided by statute, no evidence other than the writing itself is admissible to prove the content of a writing. This section shall be known and may be cited as the best evidence rule.
BEQUEST - A gift of personal property under a will.
BILL - A formal written statement of complaint to a court of justice; also, a draft of an act of the legislature before it becomes a law; also, accounts for goods sold, services rendered, or work done.
BONA FIDE - In or with good faith; honestly.
BOND - An instrument by which the maker promises to pay a sum of money to another, usually providing that upon performances of a certain condition the obligation shall be void.
BOYCOTT - A plan to prevent the carrying on of a business by wrongful means.
BREACH - The breaking or violating of a law, or the failure to carry out a duty.
BRIEF - A written document, prepared by a lawyer to serve as the basis of an argument upon a case in court, usually an appellate court.
BURDEN OF PRODUCING EVIDENCE - The obligation of a party to introduce evidence sufficient to avoid a ruling against him on the issue.
BURDEN OF PROOF - The obligation of a party to establish by evidence a requisite degree of belief concerning a fact in the mind of the trier of fact or the court. The burden of proof may require a party to raise a reasonable doubt concerning the existence of nonexistence of a fact or that he establish the existence or nonexistence of a fact by a preponderance of the evidence, by clear and convincing proof, or by proof beyond a reasonable doubt.

Except as otherwise provided by law, the burden of proof requires proof by a preponderance of the evidence.

BUSINESS, A - Shall include every kind of business, profession, occupation, calling or operation of institutions, whether carried on for profit or not.

BY-LAWS - Regulations, ordinances, or rules enacted by a corporation, association, etc., for its own government.

C

CANON - A doctrine; also, a law or rule, of a church or association in particular.

CAPIAS - An order to arrest.

CAPTION - In a pleading, deposition or other paper connected with a case in court, it is the heading or introductory clause which shows the names of the parties, name of the court, number of the case on the docket or calendar, etc.

CARRIER - A person or corporation undertaking to transport persons or property.

CASE - A general term for an action, cause, suit, or controversy before a judicial body.

CAUSE - A suit, litigation or action before a court.

CAVEAT EMPTOR - Let the buyer beware. This term expresses the rule that the purchaser of an article must examine, judge, and test it for himself, being bound to discover any obvious defects or imperfections.

CERTIFICATE - A written representation that some legal formality has been complied with.

CERTIORARI - To be informed of; the name of a writ issued by a superior court directing the lower court to send up to the former the record and proceedings of a case.

CHANGE OF VENUE - To remove place of trial from one place to another.

CHARGE - An obligation or duty; a formal complaint; an instruction of the court to the jury upon a case.

CHARTER - (n.) The authority by virtue of which an organized body acts;
  (v.) in mercantile law, it means to hire or lease a vehicle or vessel for transportation.

CHATTEL - An article of personal property.

CHATTEL MORTGAGE - A mortgage on personal property.

CIRCUIT - A division of the country, for the administration of justice; a geographical area served by a court.

CITATION - The act of the court by which a person is summoned or cited; also, a reference to legal authority.

CIVIL (ACTIONS) - It indicates the private rights and remedies of individuals in contrast to the word "criminal" (actions) which relates to prosecution for violation of laws.

CLAIM (n.) - Any demand held or asserted as of right.

CODICIL - An addition to a will.

CODIFY - To arrange the laws of a country into a code.

COGNIZANCE - Notice or knowledge.

COLLATERAL - By the side; accompanying; an article or thing given to secure performance of a promise.

COMITY - Courtesy; the practice by which one court follows the decision of another court on the same question.

COMMIT - To perform, as an act; to perpetrate, as a crime; to send a person to prison.

COMMON LAW - As distinguished from law created by the enactment of the legislature (called statutory law), it relates to those principles and rules of action which derive their authority solely from usages and customs of immemorial antiquity, particularly with reference to the ancient unwritten law of England. The written pronouncements of the common law are found in court decisions.

COMMUTE - Change punishment to one less severe.

COMPLAINANT - One who applies to the court for legal redress.
COMPLAINT - The pleading of a plaintiff in a civil action; or a charge that a person has committed a specified offense.
COMPROMISE - An arrangement for settling a dispute by agreement.
CONCUR - To agree, consent.
CONCURRENT - Running together, at the same time.
CONDEMNATION - Taking private property for public use on payment therefor.
CONDITION - Mode or state of being; a qualification or restriction.
CONDUCT - Active and passive behavior; both verbal and nonverbal.
CONFESSION - Voluntary statement of guilt of crime.
CONFIDENTIAL COMMUNICATION BETWEEN CLIENT AND LAWYER - Information transmitted between a client and his lawyer in the course of that relationship and in confidence by a means which, so far as the client is aware, discloses the information to no third persons other than those who are present to further the interest of the client in the consultation or those to whom disclosure is reasonably necessary for the transmission of the information or the accomplishment of the purpose for which the lawyer is consulted, and includes a legal opinion formed and the advice given by the lawyer in the course of that relationship.
CONFRONTATION - Witness testifying in presence of defendant.
CONSANGUINITY - Blood relationship.
CONSIGN - To give in charge; commit; entrust; to send or transmit goods to a merchant, factor, or agent for sale.
CONSIGNEE - One to whom a consignment is made.
CONSIGNOR - One who sends or makes a consignment.
CONSPIRACY - In criminal law, it means an agreement between two or more persons to commit an unlawful act.
CONSPIRATORS - Persons involved in a conspiracy.
CONSTITUTION - The fundamental law of a nation or state.
CONSTRUCTION OF GENDERS - The masculine gender includes the feminine and neuter.
CONSTRUCTION OF SINGULAR AND PLURAL - The singular number includes the plural; and the plural, the singular.
CONSTRUCTION OF TENSES - The present tense includes the past and future tenses; and the future, the present.
CONSTRUCTIVE - An act or condition assumed from other parts or conditions.
CONSTRUE - To ascertain the meaning of language.
CONSUMMATE - To complete.
CONTIGUOUS - Adjoining; touching; bounded by.
CONTINGENT - Possible, but not assured; dependent upon some condition.
CONTINUANCE - The adjournment or postponement of an action pending in a court.
CONTRA - Against, opposed to; contrary.
CONTRACT - An agreement between two or more persons to do or not to do a particular thing.
CONTROVERT - To dispute, deny.
CONVERSION - Dealing with the personal property of another as if it were one's own, without right.
CONVEYANCE - An instrument transferring title to land.
CONVICTION - Generally, the result of a criminal trial which ends in a judgment or sentence that the defendant is guilty as charged.

COOPERATIVE - A cooperative is a voluntary organization of persons with a common interest, formed and operated along democratic lines for the purpose of supplying services at cost to its members and other patrons, who contribute both capital and business.

CORPUS DELICTI - The body of a crime; the crime itself.

CORROBORATE - To strengthen; to add weight by additional evidence.

COUNTERCLAIM - A claim presented by a defendant in opposition to or deduction from the claim of the plaintiff.

COUNTY - Political subdivision of a state.

COVENANT - Agreement.

CREDIBLE - Worthy of belief.

CREDITOR - A person to whom a debt is owing by another person, called the "debtor."

CRIMINAL ACTION - Includes criminal proceedings.

CRIMINAL INFORMATION - Same as complaint.

CRITERION (sing.)

CRITERIA (plural) - A means or tests for judging; a standard or standards.

CROSS-EXAMINATION - Examination of a witness by a party other than the direct examiner upon a matter that is within the scope of the direct examination of the witness.

CULPABLE - Blamable.

CY-PRES - As near as (possible). The rule of *cy-pres* is a rule for the construction of instruments in equity by which the intention of the party is carried out *as near as may be*, when it would be impossible or illegal to give it literal effect.

D

DAMAGES - A monetary compensation, which may be recovered in the courts by any person who has suffered loss, or injury, whether to his person, property or rights through the unlawful act or omission or negligence of another.

DECLARANT - A person who makes a statement.

DE FACTO - In fact; actually but without legal authority.

DE JURE - Of right; legitimate; lawful.

DE MINIMIS - Very small or trifling.

DE NOVO - Anew; afresh; a second time.

DEBT - A specified sum of money owing to one person from another, including not only the obligation of the debtor to pay, but the right of the creditor to receive and enforce payment.

DECEDENT - A dead person.

DECISION - A judgment or decree pronounced by a court in determination of a case.

DECREE - An order of the court, determining the rights of all parties to a suit.

DEED - A writing containing a contract sealed and delivered; particularly to convey real property.

DEFALCATION - Misappropriation of funds.

DEFAMATION - Injuring one's reputation by false statements.

DEFAULT - The failure to fulfill a duty, observe a promise, discharge an obligation, or perform an agreement.

DEFENDANT - The person defending or denying; the party against whom relief or recovery is sought in an action or suit.

DEFRAUD - To practice fraud; to cheat or trick.

DELEGATE (v.)- To entrust to the care or management of another.

DELICTUS - A crime.

DEMUR (v.) - To dispute the sufficiency in law of the pleading of the other side.

DEMURRAGE - In maritime law, it means, the sum fixed or allowed as remuneration to the owners of a ship for the detention of their vessel beyond the number of days allowed for loading and unloading or for sailing; also used in railroad terminology.
DENIAL - A form of pleading; refusing to admit the truth of a statement, charge, etc.
DEPONENT - One who gives testimony under oath reduced to writing.
DEPOSITION - Testimony given under oath outside of court for use in court or for the purpose of obtaining information in preparation for trial of a case.
DETERIORATION - A degeneration such as from decay, corrosion or disintegration.
DETRIMENT - Any loss or harm to person or property.
DEVIATION - A turning aside.
DEVISE - A gift of real property by the last will and testament of the donor.
DICTUM (sing.)
DICTA (plural) - Any statements made by the court in an opinion concerning some rule of law not necessarily involved nor essential to the determination of the case.
DIRECT EVIDENCE - Evidence that directly proves a fact, without an inference or presumption, and which in itself if true, conclusively establishes that fact.
DIRECT EXAMINATION - The first examination of a witness upon a matter that is not within the scope of a previous examination of the witness.
DISAFFIRM - To repudiate.
DISMISS - In an action or suit, it means to dispose of the case without any further consideration or hearing.
DISSENT - To denote disagreement of one or more judges of a court with the decision passed by the majority upon a case before them.
DOCKET (n.) - A formal record, entered in brief, of the proceedings in a court.
DOCTRINE - A rule, principle, theory of law.
DOMICILE - That place where a man has his true, fixed and permanent home to which whenever he is absent he has the intention of returning.
DRAFT (n.) - A commercial paper ordering payment of money drawn by one person on another.
DRAWEE - The person who is requested to pay the money.
DRAWER - The person who draws the commercial paper and addresses it to the drawee.
DUPLICATE - A counterpart produced by the same impression as the original enlargements and miniatures, or by mechanical or electronic re-recording, or by chemical reproduction, or by other equivalent technique which accurately reproduces the original.
DURESS - Use of force to compel performance or non-performance of an act.

E

EASEMENT - A liberty, privilege, or advantage without profit, in the lands of another.
EGRESS - Act or right of going out or leaving; emergence.
EIUSDEM GENERIS - Of the same kind, class or nature. A rule used in the construction of language in a legal document.
EMBEZZLEMENT - To steal; to appropriate fraudulently to one's own use property entrusted to one's care.
EMBRACERY - Unlawful attempt to influence jurors, etc., but not by offering value.
EMINENT DOMAIN - The right of a state to take private property for public use.
ENACT - To make into a law.
ENDORSEMENT - Act of writing one's name on the back of a note, bill or similar written instrument.

ENJOIN - To require a person, by writ of injunction from a court of equity, to perform or to abstain or desist from some act.
ENTIRETY - The whole; that which the law considers as one whole, and not capable of being divided into parts.
ENTRAPMENT - Inducing one to commit a crime so as to arrest him.
ENUMERATED - Mentioned specifically; designated.
ENURE - To operate or take effect.
EQUITY - In its broadest sense, this term denotes the spirit and the habit of fairness, justness, and right dealing which regulate the conduct of men.
ERROR - A mistake of law, or the false or irregular application of law as will nullify the judicial proceedings.
ESCROW - A deed, bond or other written engagement, delivered to a third person, to be delivered by him only upon the performance or fulfillment of some condition.
ESTATE - The interest which any one has in lands, or in any other subject of property.
ESTOP - To stop, bar, or impede.
ESTOPPEL - A rule of law which prevents a man from alleging or denying a fact, because of his own previous act.
ET AL. (alii) - And others.
ET SEQ. (sequential) - And the following.
ET UX. (uxor) - And wife.
EVIDENCE - Testimony, writings, material objects, or other things presented to the senses that are offered to prove the existence or non-existence of a fact.
    Means from which inferences may be drawn as a basis of proof in duly constituted judicial or fact finding tribunals, and includes testimony in the form of opinion and hearsay.
EX CONTRACTU
EX DELICTO - In law, rights and causes of action are divided into two classes, those arising *ex contractu* (from a contract) and those arising *ex delicto* (from a delict or tort).
EX OFFICIO - From office; by virtue of the office.
EX PARTE - On one side only; by or for one.
EX POST FACTO - After the fact.
EX POST FACTO LAW - A law passed after an act was done which retroactively makes such act a crime.
EX REL. (relations) - Upon relation or information.
EXCEPTION - An objection upon a matter of law to a decision made, either before or after judgment by a court.
EXECUTOR (male)
EXECUTRIX (female) - A person who has been appointed by will to execute the will.
EXECUTORY - That which is yet to be executed or performed.
EXEMPT - To release from some liability to which others are subject.
EXONERATION - The removal of a burden, charge or duty.
EXTRADITION - Surrender of a fugitive from one nation to another.

F

F.A.S.- "Free alongside ship"; delivery at dock for ship named.
F.O.B.- "Free on board"; seller will deliver to car, truck, vessel, or other conveyance by which goods are to be transported, without expense or risk of loss to the buyer or consignee.
FABRICATE - To construct; to invent a false story.
FACSIMILE - An exact or accurate copy of an original instrument.

FACTOR - A commercial agent.
FEASANCE - The doing of an act.
FELONIOUS - Criminal, malicious.
FELONY - Generally, a criminal offense that may be punished by death or imprisonment for more than one year as differentiated from a misdemeanor.
FEME SOLE - A single woman.
FIDUCIARY - A person who is invested with rights and powers to be exercised for the benefit of another person.
FIERI FACIAS - A writ of execution commanding the sheriff to levy and collect the amount of a judgment from the goods and chattels of the judgment debtor.
FINDING OF FACT - Determination from proof or judicial notice of the existence of a fact. A ruling implies a supporting finding of fact; no separate or formal finding is required unless required by a statute of this state.
FISCAL - Relating to accounts or the management of revenue.
FORECLOSURE (sale) - A sale of mortgaged property to obtain satisfaction of the mortgage out of the sale proceeds.
FORFEITURE - A penalty, a fine.
FORGERY - Fabricating or producing falsely, counterfeited.
FORTUITOUS - Accidental.
FORUM - A court of justice; a place of jurisdiction.
FRAUD - Deception; trickery.
FREEHOLDER - One who owns real property.
FUNGIBLE - Of such kind or nature that one specimen or part may be used in the place of another.

G

GARNISHEE - Person garnished.
GARNISHMENT - A legal process to reach the money or effects of a defendant, in the possession or control of a third person.
GRAND JURY - Not less than 16, not more than 23 citizens of a county sworn to inquire into crimes committed or triable in the county.
GRANT - To agree to; convey, especially real property.
GRANTEE - The person to whom a grant is made.
GRANTOR - The person by whom a grant is made.
GRATUITOUS - Given without a return, compensation or consideration.
GRAVAMEN - The grievance complained of or the substantial cause of a criminal action.
GUARANTY (n.) - A promise to answer for the payment of some debt, or the performance of some duty, in case of the failure of another person, who, in the first instance, is liable for such payment or performance.
GUARDIAN - The person, committee, or other representative authorized by law to protect the person or estate or both of an incompetent (or of a *sui juris* person having a guardian) and to act for him in matters affecting his person or property or both. An incompetent is a person under disability imposed by law.
GUILTY - Establishment of the fact that one has committed a breach of conduct; especially, a violation of law.

H

HABEAS CORPUS - You have the body; the name given to a variety of writs, having for their object to bring a party before a court or judge for decision as to whether such person is being lawfully held prisoner.

HABENDUM - In conveyancing; it is the clause in a deed conveying land which defines the extent of ownership to be held by the grantee.

HEARING - A proceeding whereby the arguments of the interested parties are heared.

HEARSAY - A type of testimony given by a witness who relates, not what he knows personally, but what others have told hi, or what he has heard said by others.

HEARSAY RULE, THE - (a) "Hearsay evidence" is evidence of a statement that was made other than by a witness while testifying at the hearing and that is offered to prove the truth of the matter stated; (b) Except as provided by law, hearsay evidence is inadmissible; (c) This section shall be known and may be cited as the hearsay rule.

HEIR - Generally, one who inherits property, real or personal.

HOLDER OF THE PRIVILEGE - (a) The client when he has no guardian or conservator; (b) A guardian or conservator of the client when the client has a guardian or conservator; (c) The personal representative of the client if the client is dead; (d) A successor, assign, trustee in dissolution, or any similar representative of a firm, association, organization, partnership, business trust, corporation, or public entity that is no longer in existence.

HUNG JURY - One so divided that they can't agree on a verdict.

HUSBAND-WIFE PRIVILEGE - An accused in a criminal proceeding has a privilege to prevent his spouse from testifying against him.

HYPOTHECATE - To pledge a thing without delivering it to the pledgee.

HYPOTHESIS - A supposition, assumption, or toehry.

I

I.E. (id est) - That is.

IB., OR IBID.(ibidem) - In the same place; used to refer to a legal reference previously cited to avoid repeating the entire citation.

ILLICIT - Prohibited; unlawful.

ILLUSORY - Deceiving by false appearance.

IMMUNITY - Exemption.

IMPEACH - To accuse, to dispute.

IMPEDIMENTS - Disabilities, or hindrances.

IMPLEAD - To sue or prosecute by due course of law.

IMPUTED - Attributed or charged to.

IN LOCO PARENTIS - In place of parent, a guardian.

IN TOTO - In the whole; completely.

INCHOATE - Imperfect; unfinished.

INCOMMUNICADO - Denial of the right of a prisoner to communicate with friends or relatives.

INCOMPETENT - One who is incapable of caring for his own affairs because he is mentally deficient or undeveloped.

INCRIMINATION - A matter will incriminate a person if it constitutes, or forms an essential part of, or, taken in connection with other matters disclosed, is a basis for a reasonable inference of such a violation of the laws of this State as to subject him to liability to punishment therefor, unless he has become for any reason permanently immune from punishment for such violation.

INCUMBRANCE - Generally a claim, lien, charge or liability attached to and binding real property.

INDEMNIFY - To secure against loss or damage; also, to make reimbursement to one for a loss already incurred by him.
INDEMNITY - An agreement to reimburse another person in case of an anticipated loss falling upon him.
INDICIA - Signs; indications.
INDICTMENT - An accusation in writing found and presented by a grand jury charging that a person has committed a crime.
INDORSE - To write a name on the back of a legal paper or document, generally, a negotiable instrument
INDUCEMENT - Cause or reason why a thing is done or that which incites the person to do the act or commit a crime; the motive for the criminal act.
INFANT - In civil cases one under 21 years of age.
INFORMATION - A formal accusation of crime made by a prosecuting attorney.
INFRA - Below, under; this word occurring by itself in a publication refers the reader to a future part of the publication.
INGRESS - The act of going into.
INJUNCTION - A writ or order by the court requiring a person, generally, to do or to refrain from doing an act.
INSOLVENT - The condition of a person who is unable to pay his debts.
INSTRUCTION - A direction given by the judge to the jury concerning the law of the case.
INTERIM - In the meantime; time intervening.
INTERLOCUTORY - Temporary, not final; something intervening between the commencement and the end of a suit which decides some point or matter, but is not a final decision of the whole controversy.
INTERROGATORIES - A series of formal written questions used in the examination of a party or a witness usually prior to a trial.
INTESTATE - A person who dies without a will.
INURE - To result, to take effect.
IPSO FACTO - By the fact iself; by the mere fact.
ISSUE (n.) The disputed point or question in a case,

J

JEOPARDY - Danger, hazard, peril.
JOINDER - Joining; uniting with another person in some legal steps or proceeding.
JOINT - United; combined.
JUDGE - Member or members or representative or representatives of a court conducting a trial or hearing at which evidence is introduced.
JUDGMENT - The official decision of a court of justice.
JUDICIAL OR JUDICIARY - Relating to or connected with the administration of justice.
JURAT - The clause written at the foot of an affidavit, stating when, where and before whom such affidavit was sworn.
JURISDICTION - The authority to hear and determine controversies between parties.
JURISPRUDENCE - The philosophy of law.
JURY - A body of persons legally selected to inquire into any matter of fact, and to render their verdict according to the evidence.

L

LACHES - The failure to diligently assert a right, which results in a refusal to allow relief.

LANDLORD AND TENANT - A phrase used to denote the legal relation existing between the owner and occupant of real estate.
LARCENY - Stealing personal property belonging to another.
LATENT - Hidden; that which does not appear on the face of a thing.
LAW - Includes constitutional, statutory, and decisional law.
LAWYER-CLIENT PRIVILEGE - (1) A "client" is a person, public officer, or corporation, association, or other organization or entity, either public or private, who is rendered professional legal services by a lawyer, or who consults a lawyer with a view to obtaining professional legal services from him; (2) A "lawyer" is a person authorized, or reasonably believed by the client to be authorized, to practice law in any state or nation; (3) A "representative of the lawyer" is one employed to assist the lawyer in the rendition of professional legal services; (4) A communication is "confidential" if not intended to be disclosed to third persons other than those to whom disclosure is in furtherance of the rendition of professional legal services to the client or those reasonably necessary for the transmission of the communication.

General rule of privilege - A client has a privilege to refuse to disclose and to prevent any other person from disclosing confidential communications made for the purpose of facilitating the rendition of professional legal services to the client, (1) between himself or his representative and his lawyer or his lawyer's representative, or (2) between his lawyer and the lawyer's representative, or (3) by him or his lawyer to a lawyer representing another in a matter of common interest, or (4) between representatives of the client or between the client and a representative of the client, or (5) between lawyers representing the client.
LEADING QUESTION - Question that suggests to the witness the answer that the examining party desires.
LEASE - A contract by which one conveys real estate for a limited time usually for a specified rent; personal property also may be leased.
LEGISLATION - The act of enacting laws.
LEGITIMATE - Lawful.
LESSEE - One to whom a lease is given.
LESSOR - One who grants a lease
LEVY - A collecting or exacting by authority.
LIABLE - Responsible; bound or obligated in law or equity.
LIBEL (v.) - To defame or injure a person's reputation by a published writing.
(n.) - The initial pleading on the part of the plaintiff in an admiralty proceeding.
LIEN - A hold or claim which one person has upon the property of another as a security for some debt or charge.
LIQUIDATED - Fixed; settled.
LIS PENDENS - A pending civil or criminal action.
LITERAL - According to the language.
LITIGANT - A party to a lawsuit.
LITATION - A judicial controversy.
LOCUS - A place.
LOCUS DELICTI - Place of the crime.
LOCUS POENITENTIAE - The abandoning or giving up of one's intention to commit some crime before it is fully completed or abandoning a conspiracy before its purpose is accomplished.

M

MALFEASANCE - To do a wrongful act.
MALICE - The doing of a wrongful act Intentionally without just cause or excuse.

MANDAMUS - The name of a writ issued by a court to enforce the performance of some public duty.
MANDATORY (adj.) Containing a command.
MARITIME - Pertaining to the sea or to commerce thereon.
MARSHALING - Arranging or disposing of in order.
MAXIM - An established principle or proposition.
MINISTERIAL - That which involves obedience to instruction, but demands no special discretion, judgment or skill.
MISAPPROPRIATE - Dealing fraudulently with property entrusted to one.
MISDEMEANOR - A crime less than a felony and punishable by a fine or imprisonment for less than one year.
MISFEASANCE - Improper performance of a lawful act.
MISREPRESENTATION - An untrue representation of facts.
MITIGATE - To make or become less severe, harsh.
MITTIMUS - A warrant of commitment to prison.
MOOT (adj.) Unsettled, undecided, not necessary to be decided.
MORTGAGE - A conveyance of property upon condition, as security for the payment of a debt or the performance of a duty, and to become void upon payment or performance according to the stipulated terms.
MORTGAGEE - A person to whom property is mortgaged.
MORTGAGOR - One who gives a mortgage.
MOTION - In legal proceedings, a "motion" is an application, either written or oral, addressed to the court by a party to an action or a suit requesting the ruling of the court on a matter of law.
MUTUALITY - Reciprocation.

N

NEGLIGENCE - The failure to exercise that degree of care which an ordinarily prudent person would exercise under like circumstances.
NEGOTIABLE (instrument) - Any instrument obligating the payment of money which is transferable from one person to another by endorsement and delivery or by delivery only.
NEGOTIATE - To transact business; to transfer a negotiable instrument; to seek agreement for the amicable disposition of a controversy or case.
NOLLE PROSEQUI - A formal entry upon the record, by the plaintiff in a civil suit or the prosecuting officer in a criminal action, by which he declares that he "will no further prosecute" the case.
NOLO CONTENDERE - The name of a plea in a criminal action, having the same effect as a plea of guilty; but not constituting a direct admission of guilt.
NOMINAL - Not real or substantial.
NOMINAL DAMAGES - Award of a trifling sum where no substantial injury is proved to have been sustained.
NONFEASANCE - Neglect of duty.
NOVATION - The substitution of a new debt or obligation for an existing one.
NUNC PRO TUNC - A phrase applied to acts allowed to be done after the time when they should be done, with a retroactive effect.("Now for then.")

O

OATH - Oath includes affirmation or declaration under penalty of perjury.
OBITER DICTUM - Opinion expressed by a court on a matter not essentially involved in a case and hence not a decision; also called dicta, if plural.

OBJECT (v.) - To oppose as improper or illegal and referring the question of its propriety or legality to the court.
OBLIGATION - A legal duty, by which a person is bound to do or not to do a certain thing.
OBLIGEE - The person to whom an obligation is owed.
OBLIGOR - The person who is to perform the obligation.
OFFER (v.) - To present for acceptance or rejection.
(n.) - A proposal to do a thing, usually a proposal to make a contract.
OFFICIAL INFORMATION - Information within the custody or control of a department or agency of the government the disclosure of which is shown to be contrary to the public interest.
OFFSET - A deduction.
ONUS PROBANDI - Burden of proof.
OPINION - The statement by a judge of the decision reached in a case, giving the law as applied to the case and giving reasons for the judgment; also a belief or view.
OPTION - The exercise of the power of choice; also a privilege existing in one person, for which he has paid money, which gives him the right to buy or sell real or personal property at a given price within a specified time.
ORDER - A rule or regulation; every direction of a court or judge made or entered in writing but not including a judgment.
ORDINANCE - Generally, a rule established by authority; also commonly used to designate the legislative acts of a municipal corporation.
ORIGINAL - Writing or recording itself or any counterpart intended to have the same effect by a person executing or issuing it. An "original" of a photograph includes the negative or any print therefrom. If data are stored in a computer or similar device, any printout or other output readable by sight, shown to reflect the data accurately, is an "original."
OVERT - Open, manifest.

P

PANEL - A group of jurors selected to serve during a term of the court.
PARENS PATRIAE - Sovereign power of a state to protect or be a guardian over children and incompetents.
PAROL - Oral or verbal.
PAROLE - To release one in prison before the expiration of his sentence, conditionally.
PARITY - Equality in purchasing power between the farmer and other segments of the economy.
PARTITION - A legal division of real or personal property between one or more owners.
PARTNERSHIP - An association of two or more persons to carry on as co-owners a business for profit.
PATENT (adj.) - Evident.
(n.) - A grant of some privilege, property, or authority, made by the government or sovereign of a country to one or more individuals.
PECULATION - Stealing.
PECUNIARY - Monetary.
PENULTIMATE - Next to the last.
PER CURIAM - A phrase used in the report of a decision to distinguish an opinion of the whole court from an opinion written by any one judge.
PER SE - In itself; taken alone.
PERCEIVE - To acquire knowledge through one's senses.
PEREMPTORY - Imperative; absolute.
PERJURY - To lie or state falsely under oath.

PERPETUITY - Perpetual existence; also the quality or condition of an estate limited so that it will not take effect or vest within the period fixed by law.
PERSON - Includes a natural person, firm, association, organization, partnership, business trust, corporation, or public entity.
PERSONAL PROPERTY - Includes money, goods, chattels, things in action, and evidences of debt.
PERSONALTY - Short term for personal property.
PETITION - An application in writing for an order of the court, stating the circumstances upon which it is founded and requesting any order or other relief from a court.
PLAINTIFF - A person who brings a court action.
PLEA - A pleading in a suit or action.
PLEADINGS - Formal allegations made by the parties of their respective claims and defenses, for the judgment of the court.
PLEDGE - A deposit of personal property as a security for the performance of an act.
PLEDGEE - The party to whom goods are delivered in pledge.
PLEDGOR - The party delivering goods in pledge.
PLENARY - Full; complete.
POLICE POWER - Inherent power of the state or its political subdivisions to enact laws within constitutional limits to promote the general welfare of society or the community.
POLLING THE JURY - Call the names of persons on a jury and requiring each juror to declare what his verdict is before it is legally recorded.
POST MORTEM - After death.
POWER OF ATTORNEY - A writing authorizing one to act for another.
PRECEPT - An order, warrant, or writ issued to an officer or body of officers, commanding him or them to do some act within the scope of his or their powers.
PRELIMINARY FACT - Fact upon the existence or nonexistence of which depends the admissibility or inadmissibility of evidence. The phrase "the admissibility or inadmissibility of evidence" includes the qualification or disqualification of a person to be a witness and the existence or nonexistence of a privilege.
PREPONDERANCE - Outweighing.
PRESENTMENT - A report by a grand jury on something they have investigated on their own knowledge.
PRESUMPTION - An assumption of fact resulting from a rule of law which requires such fact to be assumed from another fact or group of facts found or otherwise established in the action.
PRIMA FACUE - At first sight.
PRIMA FACIE CASE - A case where the evidence is very patent against the defendant.
PRINCIPAL - The source of authority or rights; a person primarily liable as differentiated from "principle" as a primary or basic doctrine.
PRO AND CON - For and against.
PRO RATA - Proportionally.
PROBATE - Relating to proof, especially to the proof of wills.
PROBATIVE - Tending to prove.
PROCEDURE - In law, this term generally denotes rules which are established by the Federal, State, or local Governments regarding the types of pleading and courtroom practice which must be followed by the parties involved in a criminal or civil case.
PROCLAMATION - A public notice by an official of some order, intended action, or state of facts.

PROFFERED EVIDENCE - The admissibility or inadmissibility of which is dependent upon the existence or nonexistence of a preliminary fact.

PROMISSORY (NOTE) - A promise in writing to pay a specified sum at an expressed time, or on demand, or at sight, to a named person, or to his order, or bearer.

PROOF - The establishment by evidence of a requisite degree of belief concerning a fact in the mind of the trier of fact or the court.

PROPERTY - Includes both real and personal property.

PROPRIETARY (adj.) - Relating or pertaining to ownership; usually a single owner.

PROSECUTE - To carry on an action or other judicial proceeding; to proceed against a person criminally.

PROVISO - A limitation or condition in a legal instrument.

PROXIMATE - Immediate; nearest

PUBLIC EMPLOYEE - An officer, agent, or employee of a public entity.

PUBLIC ENTITY - Includes a national, state, county, city and county, city, district, public authority, public agency, or any other political subdivision or public corporation, whether foreign or domestic.

PUBLIC OFFICIAL - Includes an official of a political dubdivision of such state or territory and of a municipality.

PUNITIVE - Relating to punishment.

Q

QUASH - To make void.

QUASI - As if; as it were.

QUID PRO QUO - Something for something; the giving of one valuable thing for another.

QUITCLAIM (v.) - To release or relinquish claim or title to, especially in deeds to realty.

QUO WARRANTO - A legal procedure to test an official's right to a public office or the right to hold a franchise, or to hold an office in a domestic corporation.

R

RATIFY - To approve and sanction.

REAL PROPERTY - Includes lands, tenements, and hereditaments.

REALTY - A brief term for real property.

REBUT - To contradict; to refute, especially by evidence and arguments.

RECEIVER - A person who is appointed by the court to receive, and hold in trust property in litigation.

RECIDIVIST - Habitual criminal.

RECIPROCAL - Mutual.

RECOUPMENT - To keep back or get something which is due; also, it is the right of a defendant to have a deduction from the amount of the plaintiff's damages because the plaintiff has not fulfilled his part of the same contract.

RECROSS EXAMINATION - Examination of a witness by a cross-examiner subsequent to a redirect examination of the witness.

REDEEM - To release an estate or article from mortgage or pledge by paying the debt for which it stood as security.

REDIRECT EXAMINATION - Examination of a witness by the direct examiner subsequent to the cross-examination of the witness.

REFEREE - A person to whom a cause pending in a court is referred by the court, to take testimony, hear the parties, and report thereon to the court.

REFERENDUM - A method of submitting an important legislative or administrative matter to a direct vote of the people.
RELEVANT EVIDENCE - Evidence including evidence relevant to the credulity of a witness or hearsay declarant, having any tendency in reason to prove or disprove any disputed fact that is of consequence to the determination of the action.
REMAND - To send a case back to the lower court from which it came, for further proceedings.
REPLEVIN - An action to recover goods or chattels wrongfully taken or detained.
REPLY (REPLICATION) - Generally, a reply is what the plaintiff or other person who has instituted proceedings says in answer to the defendant's case.
RE JUDICATA - A thing judicially acted upon or decided.
RES ADJUDICATA - Doctrine that an issue or dispute litigated and determined in a case between the opposing parties is deemed permanently decided between these parties.
RESCIND (RECISSION) - To avoid or cancel a contract.
RESPONDENT - A defendant in a proceeding in chancery or admiralty; also, the person who contends against the appeal in a case.
RESTITUTION - In equity, it is the restoration of both parties to their original condition (when practicable), upon the rescission of a contract for fraud or similar cause.
RETROACTIVE (RETROSPECTIVE) - Looking back; effective as of a prior time.
REVERSED - A term used by appellate courts to indicate that the decision of the lower court in the case before it has been set aside.
REVOKE - To recall or cancel.
RIPARIAN (RIGHTS) - The rights of a person owning land containing or bordering on a water course or other body of water, such as lakes and rivers.

S

SALE - A contract whereby the ownership of property is transferred from one person to another for a sum of money or for any consideration.
SANCTION - A penalty or punishment provided as a means of enforcing obedience to a law; also, an authorization.
SATISFACTION - The discharge of an obligation by paying a party what is due to him; or what is awarded to him by the judgment of a court or otherwise.
SCIENTER - Knowingly; also, it is used in pleading to denote the defendant's guilty knowledge.
SCINTILLA - A spark; also the least particle.
SECRET OF STATE - Governmental secret relating to the national defense or the international relations of the United States.
SECURITY - Indemnification; the term is applied to an obligation, such as a mortgage or deed of trust, given by a debtor to insure the payment or performance of his debt, by furnishing the creditor with a resource to be used in case of the debtor's failure to fulfill the principal obligation.
SENTENCE - The judgment formally pronounced by the court or judge upon the defendant after his conviction in a criminal prosecution.
SET-OFF - A claim or demand which one party in an action credits against the claim of the opposing party.
SHALL and MAY - "Shall" is mandatory and "may" is permissive.
SITUS - Location.
SOVEREIGN - A person, body or state in which independent and supreme authority is vested.
STARE DECISIS - To follow decided cases.

STATE - "State" means this State, unless applied to the different parts of the United States. In the latter case, it includes any state, district, commonwealth, territory or insular possession of the United States, including the District of Columbia.
STATEMENT - (a) Oral or written verbal expression or (b) nonverbal conduct of a person intended by him as a substitute for oral or written verbal expression.
STATUTE - An act of the legislature. Includes a treaty.
STATUTE OF LIMITATION - A statute limiting the time to bring an action after the right of action has arisen.
STAY - To hold in abeyance an order of a court.
STIPULATION - Any agreement made by opposing attorneys regulating any matter incidental to the proceedings or trial.
SUBORDINATION (AGREEMENT) - An agreement making one's rights inferior to or of a lower rank than another's.
SUBORNATION - The crime of procuring a person to lie or to make false statements to a court.
SUBPOENA - A writ or order directed to a person, and requiring his attendance at a particular time and place to testify as a witness.
SUBPOENA DUCES TECUM - A subpoena used, not only for the purpose of compelling witnesses to attend in court, but also requiring them to bring with them books or documents which may be in their possession, and which may tend to elucidate the subject matter of the trial.
SUBROGATION - The substituting of one for another as a creditor, the new creditor succeeding to the former's rights.
SUBSIDY - A government grant to assist a private enterprise deemed advantageous to the public.
SUI GENERIS - Of the same kind.
SUIT - Any civil proceeding by a person or persons against another or others in a court of justice by which the plaintiff pursues the remedies afforded him by law.
SUMMONS - A notice to a defendant that an action against him has been commenced and requiring him to appear in court and answer the complaint.
SUPRA - Above; this word occurring by itself in a book refers the reader to a previous part of the book.
SURETY - A person who binds himself for the payment of a sum of money, or for the performance of something else, for another.
SURPLUSAGE - Extraneous or unnecessary matter.
SURVIVORSHIP - A term used when a person becomes entitled to property by reason of his having survived another person who had an interest in the property.
SUSPEND SENTENCE - Hold back a sentence pending good behavior of prisoner.
SYLLABUS - A note prefixed to a report, especially a case, giving a brief statement of the court's ruling on different issues of the case.

T

TALESMAN - Person summoned to fill a panel of jurors.
TENANT - One who holds or possesses lands by any kind of right or title; also, one who has the temporary use and occupation of real property owned by another person (landlord), the duration and terms of his tenancy being usually fixed by an instrument called "a lease."
TENDER - An offer of money; an expression of willingness to perform a contract according to its terms.
TERM - When used with reference to a court, it signifies the period of time during which the court holds a session, usually of several weeks or months duration.

TESTAMENTARY - Pertaining to a will or the administration of a will.
TESTATOR (male)
TESTATRIX (female) - One who makes or has made a testament or will.
TESTIFY (TESTIMONY) - To give evidence under oath as a witness.
TO WIT - That is to say; namely.
TORT - Wrong; injury to the person.
TRANSITORY - Passing from place to place.
TRESPASS - Entry into another's ground, illegally.
TRIAL - The examination of a cause, civil or criminal, before a judge who has jurisdiction over it, according to the laws of the land.
TRIER OF FACT - Includes (a) the jury and (b) the court when the court is trying an issue of fact other than one relating to the admissibility of evidence.
TRUST - A right of property, real or personal, held by one party for the benefit of another.
TRUSTEE - One who lawfully holds property in custody for the benefit of another.

U

UNAVAILABLE AS A WITNESS - The declarant is (1) Exempted or precluded on the ground of privilege from testifying concerning the matter to which his statement is relevant; (2) Disqualified from testifying to the matter; (3) Dead or unable to attend or to testify at the hearing because of then existing physical or mental illness or infirmity; (4) Absent from the hearing and the court is unable to compel his attendance by its process; or (5) Absent from the hearing and the proponent of his statement has exercised reasonable diligence but has been unable to procure his attendance by the court's process.
ULTRA VIRES - Acts beyond the scope and power of a corporation, association, etc.
UNILATERAL - One-sided; obligation upon, or act of one party.
USURY - Unlawful interest on a loan.

V

VACATE - To set aside; to move out.
VARIANCE - A discrepancy or disagreement between two instruments or two aspects of the same case, which by law should be consistent.
VENDEE - A purchaser or buyer.
VENDOR - The person who transfers property by sale, particularly real estate; the term "seller" is used more commonly for one who sells personal property.
VENIREMEN - Persons ordered to appear to serve on a jury or composing a panel of jurors.
VENUE - The place at which an action is tried, generally based on locality or judicial district in which an injury occurred or a material fact happened.
VERDICT - The formal decision or finding of a jury.
VERIFY - To confirm or substantiate by oath.
VEST - To accrue to.
VOID - Having no legal force or binding effect.
VOIR DIRE - Preliminary examination of a witness or a juror to test competence, interest, prejudice, etc.

W

WAIVE - To give up a right.
WAIVER - The intentional or voluntary relinquishment of a known right.
WARRANT (WARRANTY) (v.) - To promise that a certain fact or state of facts, in relation to the subject matter, is, or shall be, as it is represented to be.

WARRANT (n.) - A writ issued by a judge, or other competent authority, addressed to a sheriff, or other officer, requiring him to arrest the person therein named, and bring him before the judge or court to answer or be examined regarding the offense with which he is charged.

WRIT - An order or process issued in the name of the sovereign or in the name of a court or judicial officer, commanding the performance or nonperformance of some act.

WRITING - Handwriting, typewriting, printing, photostating, photographing and every other means of recording upon any tangible thing any form of communication or representation, including letters, words, pictures, sounds, or symbols, or combinations thereof.

WRITINGS AND RECORDINGS - Consists of letters, words, or numbers, or their equivalent, set down by handwriting, typewriting, printing, photostating, photographing, magnetic impulse, mechanical or electronic recording, or other form of data compilation.

Y

YEA AND NAY - Yes and no.

YELLOW DOG CONTRACT - A contract by which employer requires employee to sign an instrument promising as condition that he will not join a union during its continuance, and will be discharged if he does join.

Z

ZONING - The division of a city by legislative regulation into districts and the prescription and application in each district of regulations having to do with structural and architectural designs of buildings and of regulations prescribing use to which buildings within designated districts may be put.